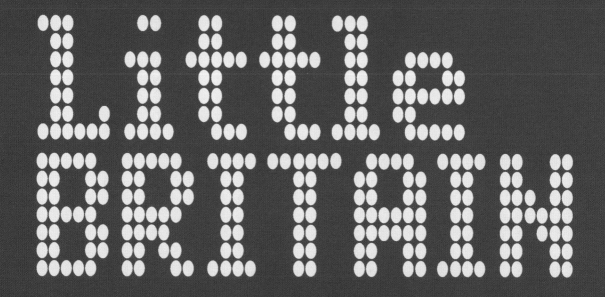

Little
BRITAIN

Written by

MATT LUCAS
AND
DAVID WALLIAMS

Britain, Britain, Britain.

Opened by the Queen in 1972, Britain now attracts hundreds of visitors a year. But why do they come? Not just to discover how chicken nuggets should really taste, or to take part in the great British tradition of dogging. No, they come in their droves to meet the people of Britain. And it is them what we now here look at now today.

LET'S ROCK!

HarperCollins*Entertainment*
An imprint of HarperCollins*Publishers*
77–85 Fulham Palace Road,
Hammersmith, London W6 8JB

www.harpercollins.co.uk

Published by HarperCollins*Entertainment* 2005
1 3 5 7 9 8 6 4 2

Matt Lucas and David Walliams assert the moral
right to be identified as the authors of this work

Design by Harry Green

A catalogue record for this book
is available from the British Library

ISBN 0 00 719872 8

Set in Rotis and Alzidienz

Printed and bound in Italy by L.E.G.O. SpA

Photographs on pages 27, 28, 35, 36, 37, 63, 64, 68, 70,
72, 74, 78, 80, 93, 96, 109, 115 (right), 127, 130, 131,
132, 139, 141, 151, 155, 156, 166, 173, 184, 192, 204,
206, 207, 215, 216, 218, 233, 237 © BBC Picture Library

All other photographs
© David Walliams and Lisa Cavalli-Green

Special spreads art direction by Roger Hammond
with photography by onEdition.com

Photographs on pp 11, 22–23 © Getty Images

Illustration by Chris Lloyd, Kuo Kang Chen
and Phosphorart

Britain, Britain, Britain, cultural capital of the world. The Sistine Chapel, British. Mozart's Requiem, British. The Great Wall of China, British. But none of that stuff would have even been invented were it not for the people of Britain, the men, the women, the boys, the girls and the monkey children that populate this well fit country, lets 'ave it!

COMA VICTIM

'Why I condemned my beautiful wife to death'

pregnancy mix-up!

Celebs • Real Lives • Lifestyle • TV Guide

R

spotted

they can't ... get away from u

- **Anne** in nightdress and slippers in a park, defecating on a squirrel.
- FatFighters' **Marjorie Dawes** continuously driving round and round the McDonald's Drive-In, Northcott.
- **Sebastian Love** sitting alone in the corner of the House Of Commons bar, weeping into his gin and tonic.
- **Bubbles DeVere** walking down Piccadilly Circus, naked.
- Little Britain star **Matt Lucas** having a full perm at Toni&Guy in Knightsbridge.
- **Vicky Pollard** flouting her ASBO and shoplifting in Oxfam, Broadmeads.
- Carer **Lou** wheeling friend Andy round Herby Cemetery, visiting Lou's mum's grave whilst

Bubbles DeVere
jogging at the Grange Hill health club

Andy complained that it was 'boring'.
- **Emily** and **Florence** at B&Q asking if they sell 'a ladies' powerdrill'.
- Scottish hotelier **Ray McCooney** wandering round the highlands and asking strangers why he wasn't in series 2.

this week's top spot!
The man who looks like **Mr T** at Heathrow Airport saying he won't get on no plane, fool.

- **Daffyd Thomas** stopping a milkman in Llandewi Breffi and asking for a pint of gay milk.

Emily in a chemist buying a bottle of Old Spice

- Little Britain star **Davi Walliams** strolling down Old Compton Street with latest flame **Dale Winton**.
- **Harvey Pincher** being breast-fed in the interval of 'Don Giovanni' at the Roya Opera House, Covent Garden.
- **Kenny Craig** outside Dixons attempting to hypnotize a parking meter into giving him his 50p back.
- University tutor **Linda Greer** waiting outside an Equal Opportunities Tribunal.
- **Maggie Blackamoor** outside Pox Village Church, vomiting over an asylum seeker.
- MidWest Bank employee **Carol Beer** coughing in the face of a pregnant woman.

Vicky Pollard
givin' evils

acknowledgements

Matt and David would like to thank everyone who appeared in series two – Tom Baker, Anthony Head, Geraldine James, Ruth Madoc, Nigel Havers, Ruth Jones, Paul Putner, Steve Furst, Samantha Power, Vanessa Feltz and everyone else who appeared, including Jaygann Ayeh, Robert Blythe, Marlon Bulger, Joanna Burford, James Cash, Charubala Chokshi, Joanne Condon, Michael Elliott, Howell Evans, Kerry Foxe, David Foxxe, Stirling Gallacher, David Garfield, Georgie Glen, Mike Hayward, Kobna Holdbrook-Smith, Cherylee Houston, Patricia Kane, Faith Kent, Geoff Leesley, Janette Legge, Joan Linder, Jennie Lucey, David Morris, Ted Robbins, Leelo Ross and Antonia Whillans.

Thanks also to everyone who worked on the show, including our stunt co-ordinator Andreas Petrides, Dean Humphrey (prop master) and the prop team (Keith Warwick, Leo Thompson, John Paul Rock, Simon Naylor and John Helmsley), our vision mixer Barbara Hicks, Andrew Gates (art director), our dubbing mixer Rob Butler-Biggs, Kelly James and Sarah Hollingsworth and the production team, production co-ordinator Charlotte Lamb, script supervisors Chrissie Bibby (thanks also to Katie Collins), our editor Mykola Pawluk, production manager and cub scout choirmaster Francis Gilson, director of photography Francis de Groote, the greatest production designer in the land – Dennis de Groote (no relation), production buyer Jac Hymen, our brilliant costume designer Annie Hardinge and her team (Sheena Gunn, Tami French and the tireless Aaron Timpali), Bronwyn at the Business, the BBC Costume Store, Angels and, of course, Chris de Witt and all at Carlo Manzi's, our wonderful make-up designer Lisa Cavalli-Green and her team (Nicola Coleman and Suzi Munachen), BBC Wigstore, Richard Mawbury and all at Wig Specialities, on cameras . . . Dave Bowden, Peter Welch, the camera team (Joe Smyth, Jonathan Tomes and Jimmy Ward), Alex Thompson, St Clair David and Jem Whippey in the sound dept, Thomas Howard and Caroline McCarthy for finding all the locations, David Arnold (who done all the music), our script editor Rob Brydon, Ted Robbins for studio warm-ups, stage manager Caroline Caley, Abi, Ollie, our ever-smiling studio resource manager Michael 'Sticky' Matheson, 1st AD Sam Dawking, 2nd AD Bart Bailey and our 3rd AD, Paul Cathie, executive producers Myfanwy Moore and Jon Plowman, lovely Matt Lipsey for directing the whole thing, and last but not least, our fantastic producer Geoff Posner. We'd also like to say thanks to our agents Connor and Melanie, Barbara, Moira and all at MBC and BBC Publicity, and to Stuart Murphy at BBC3 and Lorraine Heggessey at BBC1 for allowing us to dress up as ladies and do silly voices on your otherwise reputable channels.

Goodfly.

ANTHONY '*tony head*' HEAD

Dear Reader,

It is a great honour for me to be asked to write the foreword to this book.

I first became involved in 'Little Britain' when I appeared in the pilot episode in 2002.
At that time I was playing one of the lead characters in 'Buffy The Vampire Slayer', a hugely
successful, long-running primetime American TV series. My initial response was of course to
say 'no', but Lucas and Walliams informed me that they were in possession of a photograph of
me with my finger in an otter – an episode of my life which I deeply regret – and I was
obliged to say 'yes'. From there, the weekly humiliation began.

They would put me in a suit, tell me I was the Prime Minister, and then David Walliams
would come in and gay me up for the amusement of a crowd. To this day, Walliams maintains he
is heterosexual but trust me, he gives a bloody good impression of being otherwise. 'Oh yes,
Tony. We've just written a sketch where I rub myself up against you and, at the end, kiss you
passionately.' Ha bloody ha. Apparently they've written a bit in the next series where he
actually enters me, while Lucas watches.

What is this obsession that Lucas and Walliams have with bumbanditry? Every character in this
God-forsaken show is either a woman, a gay, or both. I digress. This show has brought shame
upon me and my family. I can no longer get work and people spit at me in the street.

I can do other things. I'm actually a really good actor. I was in 'Fat Slags – The Movie' and
'Woof!'. And 'Woof 2 – Woof Again: Why Me?' which was about a boy who turns into a dog
and is much better than it sounds. Oh yeah, and I was in 'Howard's Way', the thing about
boats so… you know, please give me a chance.

I beg you.

Yours,

Anthony Head

ANTHONY HEAD

PS. I didn't even write this. Lucas and Walliams did.

EPISODE one

TOM V/O: Britain, Britain, Britain. Opened by the Queen in 1972, Britain now attracts hundreds of visitors a year. But why do they come? Not just to discover how chicken nuggets should really taste, or to take part in the great British tradition of dogging. No, they come in their drove to meet the people of Britain. And it is them what we now here look at now today. Let's rock!

VICKY POLLARD – SUPERMARKET

EXT: SUPERMARKET. WE SEE VICKY POLLARD WITH A PRAM BEING ESCORTED OUT OF THE SUPERMARKET EXIT BY A SECURITY GUARD. VICKY IMMEDIATELY LOOPS BACK AND RE-ENTERS THE SUPERMARKET THROUGH THE ENTRANCE.

TOM V/O: Vicky Pollard is well known in her local supermarket, and is on first name terms with most of the security staff.

INT: SUPERMARKET. VICKY IS ATTEMPTING TO STEAL SWEETS FROM THE PIC-N-MIX AISLE BY PUTTING THEM DOWN THE WAISTBAND OF HER TROUSERS. WITH MOST OF THE SWEETS SPILLING ONTO THE FLOOR, VICKY LOOKS UP AND NOTICES THE SECURITY GUARD WATCHING HER.

VICKY: What are you looking at, pervert?

SECURITY GUARD: I told you before, you've got to put the pic-n-mix in a bag.

VICKY: God you're so racist.

VICKY BEGINS TO PUT SWEETS INTO A BAG AS THE SECURITY GUARD LOOKS ON.

VICKY: Alright now?!

VICKY PUTS THE WHOLE BAG DOWN HER TROUSERS.

SECURITY GUARD: Are you going to pay for those?

VICKY: No but yeah but no but yeah because I was just about to do it if you had waited. God this is so unfair I ain't ever even nicked nuffin' or nuffin' this is like being back at borstal honestly if anyone's nicked anything it's Michelle Pope because we were all at the leisure centre and Michelle Pope put her hand up the chocolate machine to try and pinch a packet of Paynes Poppets but she got her hand stuck in I tried to cut it off with a pen knife and she completely had an eppy and said that Mr Bailey was right I am educationally subnormal but anyway don't listen to her because everyone knows she done it with an Alsatian.

SECURITY GUARD: Ok, I think it's time to go now.

NobutyeahbutnobutyeahbecauseIwas justabouttodoitifyouhadwaited.Godthisis sounfairIain'teverevennickednuffin'or nuffin'thisislikebeingbackatborsta honestlyifanyone'snickedanythingit's MichellePopebecausewewereallatthe leisurecentreandMichellePopeputherhand upthechocolatemachinetotryandpincha packetofPaynesPoppetsbutshegother handstuckinItriedtocutitoffwithapen knifeandshecompletelyhadaneppyandsaid atMrBaileywasrightIameducationallysubnormal butanywaydon'tlistentoherbecause everyoneknowsshedoneitwithanAlsatian.

Don'tworryIwasgoinganywayevenbeforeyoujustsaid

thatbecauseIlikewellhatethisshopbecauseBethanyRay

gotaSaturdayjobhereandsomeonefoundadeadratin

thechocolateraisinsandsomebodythoughtitwasachocolate

andtheyboughtitandateitandcamebackthenextweekand

sayshaveyougotanymoreofthosechocolateratsandthat'strue

IswearonDuncanoutofBlue'slife.

VICKY WALKS TOWARDS THE EXIT WITH HER PRAM, ESCORTED BY THE SECURITY GUARD.

VICKY: Don't worry I was going anyway even before you just said that because I like well hate this shop because Bethany Ray got a Saturday job here and someone found a dead rat in the chocolate raisins and somebody thought it was a chocolate and they bought it and ate it and came back the next week and says have you got any more of those chocolate rats and that's true I swear on Duncan out of Blue's life.

AS VICKY LEAVES THE SUPERMARKET, SHE SETS OFF A BEEPING ALARM.

SECURITY GUARD: Can you come back in, please?

VICKY GOES BACK INTO THE SUPERMARKET.

VICKY: Oh my God this is well harassment, I'm going to take this to the court of humapean rights.

SECURITY GUARD: Lift up your arms.

THE SECURITY GUARD BEGINS TO SEARCH VICKY.

VICKY: You're only doing this because you're in love with me and you're trying to like gay me up. This is well out of order, see, totally innocent. I N A innocent.

THE SECURITY GUARD PULLS BACK THE PRAM'S BABY BLANKET TO REVEAL A TILL FULL OF MONEY.

SECURITY GUARD: What's this?

VICKY: (GUILTILY) I bought that earlier.

EMILY AND FLORENCE – CAFE

EXT. PIER. EMILY AND FLORENCE ARE ON A TANDEM, GREETING PASSERSBY AS THEY CYCLE ALONG THE SEAFRONT.

EMILY: Morning!

FLORENCE: Afternoon!

EMILY: Morning!

TOM V/O: These men are transvestites and prefer to dress as ladies. I myself am happy in both male and female clothing, as I was born without genitals.

WE SEE EMILY AND FLORENCE CYCLING TOWARDS A TEA SHOP.

EMILY: Morning!

FLORENCE: Afternoon!

EMILY: Two ladies on a bicyclette, that is all.

FLORENCE: Pay no heed.

EMILY AND FLORENCE STOP OUTSIDE THE TEA SHOP TO DISCUSS TACTICS BEFORE GOING IN.

EMILY: Now. Florence, my dear, remember we are two ladies taking afternoon tea.

FLORENCE: Yes, Emily.

EMILY: I know this is all very new to you but the trick is not to draw attention to yourself.

INT: TEA SHOP. EMILY AND FLORENCE BURST IN.

EMILY: (LOUDLY) Two ladies for tea, please.

WAITER: Yes of course, this way.

EMILY: Ladies first.

FLORENCE: I am also a lady.

EMILY: Oh yes.

THE WAITER SHOWS EMILY AND FLORENCE TO A TABLE.

WAITER: Here we are.

EMILY: Florence, do take a seat.

FLORENCE: No, after you, Emily.

I know this is all very new to you but the trick is not to draw attention to yourself.

EPISODE

EMILY: Florence, I insist.

FLORENCE: No Emily, please.

EMILY: We're both ladies, who sits first?

WITH THE WAITER WATCHING, EMILY AND FLORENCE BOB UP AND DOWN REPEATEDLY..

EMILY: (IN AN ORDINARY BLOKE'S VOICE, EXASPERATED BY THE DEADLOCK) Sit down.

THE WAITER HANDS MENUS TO EMILY AND FLORENCE.

EMILY: Merci.

FLORENCE: Thank you.

Oh yes, we are most definitely two of them, yes.

THEY LOOK AROUND AND RAISE THEIR VOICES TO MAKE SURE THAT THE OTHER CUSTOMERS CAN HEAR HOW LADYLIKE THEIR CONVERSATION IS.

EMILY: Oh Florence, regardez le menu, so many delicious foods and drinks that a lady might enjoy.

FLORENCE: Yes it all looks so nice doesn't it, my lady friend, I don't know what to have. Will you be having cake?

EMILY: If they have a lady's cake then yes, but only if, we are ladies, aren't we?

FLORENCE: Oh yes, we are most definitely two of them, yes.

EMILY: Ladies.

FLORENCE: Why don't you order for both of us, I'm off to powder my nose.

EMILY SEES FLORENCE ABOUT TO ENTER THE MEN'S TOILETS.

EMILY: (STAGE WHISPER) Other door.

FLORENCE: (LAUGHING GIRLISHLY) Oh yes.

EMILY: (LOUDLY) And don't forget to sit down when you piss.

EVERYBODY IN THE TEA SHOP STOPS AND LOOKS UP. FLORENCE IS LEFT STANDING, EMBARRASSED, BY THE TOILET DOOR.

Call me Bubbles

BUBBLES DEVERE — HEALTH SPA

EXT: HEALTH SPA. WE SEE A SIGN – 'HILL GRANGE HEALTH SPA'.

TOM V/O: At this health spa in Trump, the manager is keen to have a word with one of the guests.

THE MANAGER, MR HUTTON, IS FOLLOWING BUBBLES AS SHE WALKS DETERMINEDLY DOWN THE PATH TO HER NEXT TREATMENT.

MR HUTTON: Mrs DeVere. Sorry, Mrs DeVere . . .

BUBBLES: Call me Bubbles, everybody does.

MR HUTTON: Can I have a word?

BUBBLES: Do you mind if we walk and talk, darling, I have an algae wrap at three?

MR HUTTON: Yes, it's really just about this payment situation. You've been with us for over five months now and we still haven't received anything.

BUBBLES: Well that's terrible, terrible darling, it's outrageous, has my husband still not sent the cheque?

MR HUTTON: No I'm afraid not, we can't seem to track him down.

BUBBLES: Have you tried him on the Monte Carlo number, darling?

MR HUTTON: No, I don't have it.

BUBBLES: Have you got a pen, darling?

MR HUTTON: Um, yeah.

BUBBLES: The number is: one two, three four five, six seven, eight nine, ok, darling?

BUBBLES STARTS RUNNING UP THE STAIRS LEADING TO THE SPA. MR HUTTON HURRIES AFTER HER.

MR HUTTON: Mrs DeVere . . .

INT: HEALTH SPA. MR HUTTON IS FOLLOWING BUBBLES DOWN THE CORRIDOR.

MR HUTTON: Mrs DeVere!

INT: TREATMENT ROOM. A BEAUTY THERAPIST IS ABOUT TO DEAL WITH A CUSTOMER, WHO IS LYING ON A TREATMENT TABLE. BUBBLES SWEEPS INTO THE ROOM.

everybody does.

BUBBLES: Hello, Gita (PUSHES THE CUSTOMER OFF THE BED AND ONTO THE FLOOR) – my turn now, darling.

BEAUTY THERAPIST: Oh Miss Bubble, you're next door.

BUBBLES: (ADDRESSING THE CUSTOMER ON THE FLOOR, OUT OF SHOT) Sorry, darling, see you at dinner. (TURNS TO MR HUTTON) Never, never, never let this girl go. *Naughty*! What she does with grape nuts is pure poetry.

BUBBLES WALKS OUT AND INTO ANOTHER ROOM, MR HUTTON FOLLOWING HER.

MR HUTTON: We need to resolve this now.

BUBBLES: Very well Mr Hutton, then we shall resolve it.

BUBBLES PUSHES HIM INTO A CHAIR, WALKS OVER TO THE DOOR AND SHUTS IT. SHE TURNS THE LOCK.

BUBBLES: Are you a married man, Mr Hutton?

MR HUTTON: Yes, I am.

BUBBLES: And yet you allow yourself to be alone in a room with a rather beautiful woman. That's very *dangereuse,* don't you think?

MR HUTTON: I just really need the cheque.

BUBBLES: Very clever, darling.

BUBBLES PUTS ON SOME MUSIC, TURNS TO FACE MR HUTTON AND PROVOCATIVELY TAKES OFF HER TOWEL. SHE IS NOW COMPLETELY NAKED.

BUBBLES: I'm sure we can come to some sort of *arrangement,* Mr Hutton.

BUBBLES WALKS SLOWLY OVER TO MR HUTTON AND CLUTCHES HIS HEAD TO HER BREAST.

NEVER, NEVER, NEVER let this girl go.

Naughty! What she does with grape

nuts is pure poetry.

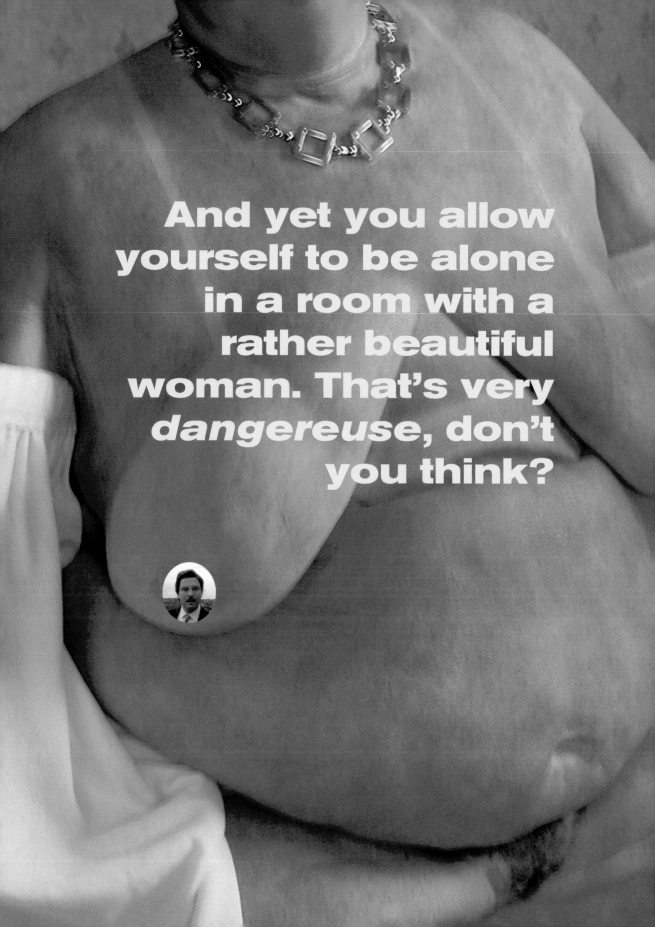

LOU AND ANDY — THE PRICE IS RIGHT

EXT: LOU IS PUSHING ANDY ALONG IN HIS WHEELCHAIR, OUTSIDE A BLOCK OF FLATS.

TOM V/O: It's a quarter to half past five and Lou is taking Andy back home from the shops.

LOU HAS STOPPED TO TALK TO A NEIGHBOUR. ANDY SNEEZES INTO HIS HANDS, TURNS AND WIPES THEM CLEAN ON THE NEIGHBOUR'S TROUSERS. EMBARRASSED, LOU WHEELS ANDY INTO THE BLOCK OF FLATS.

INT: ANDY'S FLAT. ANDY HAS JUST EATEN HIS DINNER, AND IS WATCHING *THE PRICE IS RIGHT* ON TELLY. LOU BRINGS THROUGH A CUP OF TEA FROM THE KITCHEN.

LOU: Did you enjoy that?

ANDY: (SHRUGS) Alright . . .

LOU: Oh look, it's your favourite, *The Price is Right*.

ANDY: Yeah, I know.

BRUCE FORSYTH (on TV): It's always nice to meet the stars of our show, whoever you are!

LOU: (HEADING BACK TO THE KITCHEN) I'll get started on the washing up.

BRUCE CALLS OUT VARIOUS NAMES TO WILD CHEERING; THEN LOU, WHO IS STILL WASHING UP, HEARS BRUCE SAYING 'ANDY PIPKIN, COME ON DOWN!' LOU SHAKES HIS HEAD IN DISBELIEF, BUT ON THE TV WE SEE ANDY RUNNING DOWN THE STAIRS, WAVING HIS ARMS WILDLY.

O/S: You are the first four contestants on *The Price is Right!*

ANDY (ON SCREEN): Yeah, I know.

MAGGIE AND JUDY — JAM

EXT: STALLS AT A SUMMER FETE.

TOM V/O: One thing this country does better than all the others is fetes; we can proudly boast that Britain is the fete capital of the world.

MAGGIE AND JUDY ARE MAKING THEIR WAY OVER TO A STALL COVERED IN DIFFERENT JARS OF HOMEMADE JAM.

MAGGIE: That's cakes done now, what's next, Judy?

JUDY: Next, Maggie, is jams.

MAGGIE: Jams, jolly good, thank you, Judy. (JUDY PASSES SOME JAM TO MAGGIE TO TASTE) Now what's this? Oh, plum; not my favourite conserve, Judy.

JUDY: Nor mine, Maggie.

MAGGIE: But we soldier on. Right, mmm, it's actually not bad for a plum. Actually rather good, who made this?

JUDY: Um, Emma Shepherd.

MAGGIE: Who?

JUDY: Emma Shepherd, the one who ran off with the schoolmistress.

MAGGIE BEGINS TO RETCH, AND THEN VOMITS A LITTLE ONTO THE FLOOR.

JUDY: Are you alright, Maggie?

MAGGIE: Please, Judy, no more lesbian jam. I can't keep it down.

JUDY: I'm so sorry, Maggie, I'll make a note.

JUDY DOES SO.

MAGGIE: Now, I'm assuming this is raspberry, it's not properly labelled. (JUDY PASSES HER SOME MORE JAM TO TASTE) Thank you. Mmm, that's not unpleasant, who made this?

JUDY: (LOOKING AT CLIPBOARD) Um, Sarah Tennant.

MAGGIE: Remind me.

JUDY: Sarah Tennant, the one who was married to the man who (MOUTHS) IS BLACK.

MAGGIE: I'm sorry?

JUDY: She married someone who (MOUTHS) IS BLACK.

MAGGIE: She did what?

JUDY: She married a black man.

MAGGIE VOMITS ONTO THE FLOOR.

MAGGIE: Ah Judy, you could have warned me.

JUDY: I'm so sorry, Maggie. Do . . . do you want to carry on?

Please, Judy, no more lesbian jam. I can't keep it down.

EPISODE

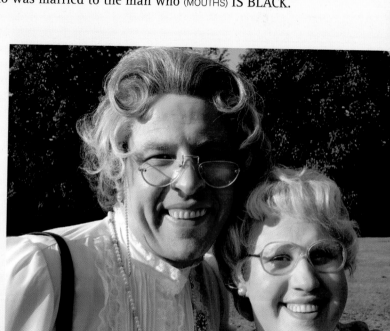

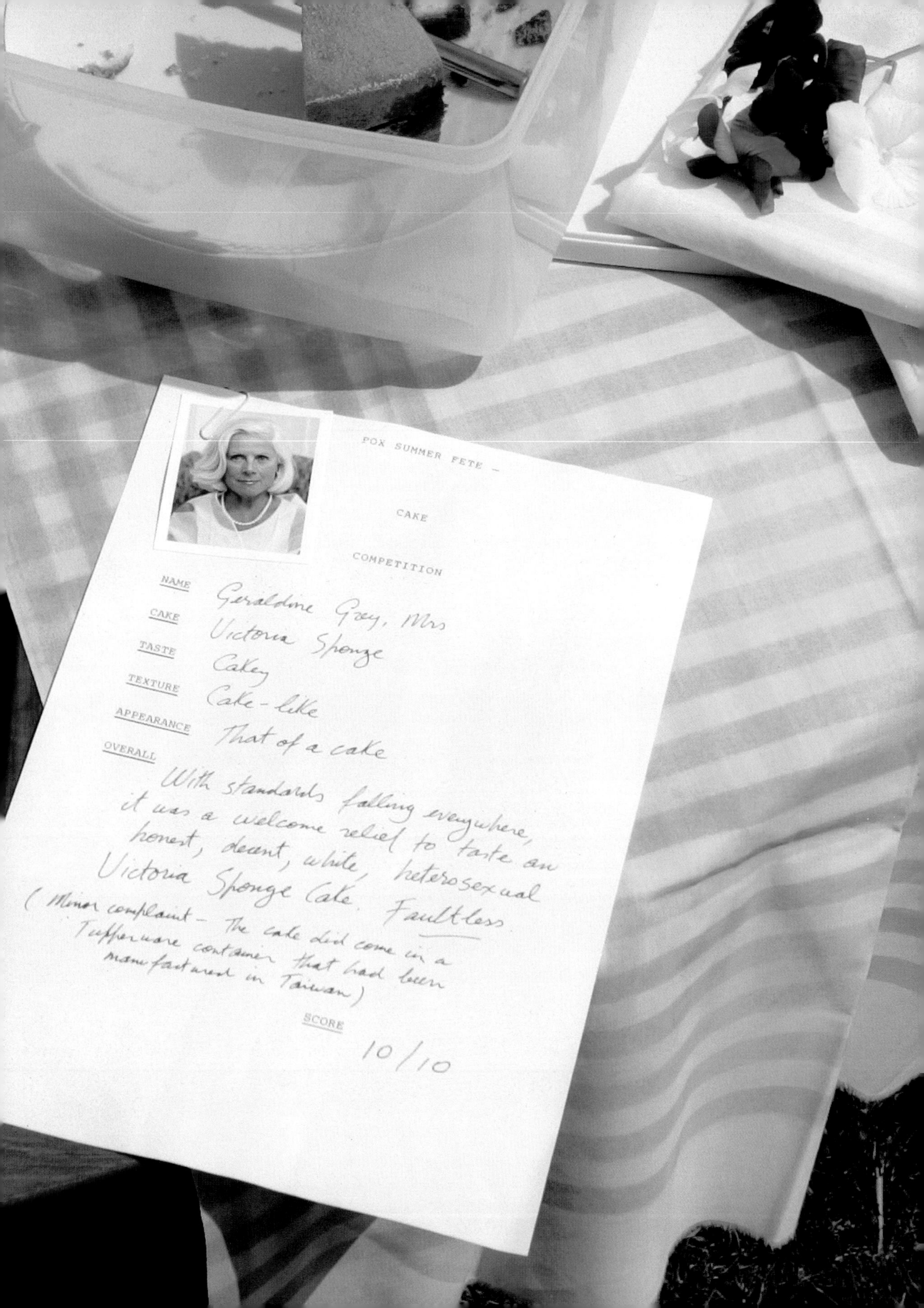
POX SUMMER FETE –
CAKE
COMPETITION
NAME Geraldine Grey, Mrs
CAKE Victoria Sponge
TASTE Cakey
TEXTURE Cake-like
APPEARANCE That of a cake
OVERALL
With standards falling everywhere, it was a welcome relief to taste an honest, decent, white, heterosexual Victoria Sponge Cake. Faultless
(Minor complaint – The cake did come in a Tupperware container that had been manufactured in Taiwan)
SCORE
10/10

MAGGIE: Yes, yes, we've got to get this done.

JUDY PASSES YET ANOTHER JAM TO MAGGIE TO TASTE.

JUDY: Right, well next, Maggie, we have a breakfast marmalade.

MAGGIE: Mmm, mmm, very nice, mmm, quite tangy, yes put down 'tangy'.

JUDY MAKES A NOTE ON HER CLIPBOARD.

JUDY: 'Tangy'.

MAGGIE: Mmm, very nice, who made this?

JUDY: (CHECKS HER NOTES) Sanjana Patel.

MAGGIE VOMITS ONTO THE FLOOR, PAUSES FOR A FEW SECONDS AND THEN VOMITS AGAIN.

MAGGIE: Right, that's jams done, then. Next, pastries.

MAGGIE TURNS FROM THE JAM TABLE AND HEADS OFF; JUDY STEPS OVER MAGGIE'S (UNSEEN) SICK
AND FOLLOWS HER.

DAFFYD – COMING OUT

EXT: WELSH VILLAGE. WE SEE THE LOCAL POSTMAN WALKING UP THE DRIVE TO
DAFFYD'S HOUSE.

TOM V/O: In the small mining village of Llandewi Breffi lies
the home of homosexual gay Daffyd Thomas.

POSTMAN: (CALLING UP TO A BEDROOM WINDOW) Morning, Daffyd!

THE CURTAINS TWITCH OPEN AND DAFFYD APPEARS WITH A LOUD HAILER.

DAFFYD: Gay rights now!

THE POSTMAN WALKS OFF.

INT: DAFFYD'S HOUSE. DAFFYD'S DAD IS SITTING AT THE TABLE, READING THE
PAPER. DAFFYD'S MUM IS BUSY IRONING.

DAFFYD'S DAD: It says here there was a bucket stole in the village on Tuesday.

DAFFYD'S MUM: Oh, it's a crime wave.

DAFFYD ENTERS ROOM.

DAFFYD: Ma, Da.

DAFFYD'S MUM & DAD: Morning, son.

DAFFYD: There's something important I have to tell you both.

DAFFYD'S MUM: Put your paper down, Dad. Now, what is it you want to say?

DAFFYD: Now you know I haven't really had any girlfriends . . .

DAFFYD'S DAD: Oh, you used to go out with that girl from the abattoir.

DAFFYD: (HOLDING UP HIS HAND TO STOP HIS FATHER SPEAKING) Yes, that was just a phase, please don't mention that again.

DAFFYD'S MUM: What about the girl at school, the one with the lazy eye? I thought you were quite taken with her.

DAFFYD: Again, the folly of youth. (GIVES A DISMISSIVE WAVE) No, what I have to tell you both is that I am – (TAKES A BIG BREATH)

DAFFYD'S DAD: Asthmatic?

DAFFYD: No, I am . . . a gay. (EMITS A CRY OF ANGUISH) Ah!

DAFFYD STAYS STANDING, IN SHOCK AT THE MAGNITUDE OF HIS OWN ANNOUNCEMENT.

DAFFYD'S MUM: (TURNING BACK TO HER IRONING) Oh that's nice, dear.

DAFFYD'S DAD: (TURNING BACK TO HIS NEWSPAPER) Yeah, good for you, lad. Oh it says here that the bucket had a chrome handle.

Again, the folly of youth. No, what I have to tell you both is that I am . . . a gay.

DAFFYD'S MUM: Oh.

DAFFYD: So you don't mind?

DAFFYD'S DAD: No.

DAFFYD: So you're not going to disown me, or cast me asunder?

DAFFYD'S MUM: Eh, oh no, to be honest, love, we did have an inkling.

SHE PICKS UP A RED STUDDED BELT OF DAFFYD'S, AND BEGINS TO POLISH IT ABSENT-MINDEDLY.

DAFFYD'S DAD: So have you got a boyfriend, then?

DAFFYD: No.

DAFFYD'S MUM: Have you not had any arse action at all?

DAFFYD: No. But I have been thinking about it, which may shock you.

DAFFYD'S MUM: Oh, well we'll have to try and fix you up with someone.

DAFFYD: Well that won't be very easy as I am the only gay in the village.

DAFFYD'S DAD: Come to think of it there's a right handsome lad who works down the mine, he takes it up the chuff.

DAFFYD: No thank you.

DAFFYD'S MUM: I know who's mad for cock. That chap who runs the sauna, you know, Gay Aled.

DAFFYD: Gay Aled is not gay.

DAFFYD'S DAD: Your Uncle Glyn's had him. Apparently he's very into water sports.

DAFFYD'S MUM: Ah, that's nice for them.

DAD SMILES IN AGREEMENT.

DAFFYD: Anyway what I think we should do is invite the whole family around here on Sunday and I can tell them all then. I don't expect they'll like it, but it's time they knew.

DAFFYD'S MUM: Oh, I don't think this Sunday is going to be much good. Your Uncle Gareth, he's gone to San Francisco.

DAFFYD'S DAD: Yeah, your cousin Bryn is going to Neath to watch Shirley Bassey.

DAFFYD: What about Auntie Sioned?

DAFFYD'S MUM: Oh no, she just stays in on a Sunday and eats minge.

DAFFYD FLOUNCES OUT OF THE ROOM AGHAST.

> # Come to think of it there's a right handsome lad who works down the mine, he takes it up the chuff.

MARJORIE DAWES/FATFIGHTERS — VANESSA FELTZ

INT: FATFIGHTERS CLUB. THE CAMERA PANS PAST A RANGE OF FATFIGHTERS PROJECTS, TO REVEAL MARJORIE WEIGHING PAT ON THE SCALES.

TOM V/O: When I see a fat person in the street I spit on them as I would a dog, and would encourage you to do the same.

MARJORIE: Ahh, you've put on three grams. You've been noshing again, haven't you? Next time you feel peckish, have a bit of dust, yeah? Alright, do you want to waddle back to your seat. (ADDRESSING THE OTHER FATFIGHTERS IN THEIR SEATS) Now, those of you who read the FatFighters newsletter will be aware that FatFighters has got a noo spokesperson, and we're very lucky because she's paying a visit to our branch tonight, so will you please give a warm welcome to . . . Vanessa Feltz! (VANESSA ENTERS THE ROOM TO APPLAUSE FROM THE MEMBERS) Vanessa. Vanessa Feltz, (MARJORIE AND VANESSA AIR-KISS) my good friend Vanessa Feltz, from the television. Come and sit down next to me, Vanessa Feltz. (MARJORIE TAKES VANESSA'S HAND) So Vanessa Feltz, you, and I know you won't mind me saying it, you were fat. (VANESSA NODS SERIOUSLY) No, we're all friends here, we can say it, and then you lost it all, didn't you?

VANESSA TURNS TO ADDRESS THE FATFIGHTERS.

VANESSA: Well the thing is, I was going through a traumatic divorce at the time –

MARJORIE: Yeah and then you piled it back on didn't you, I saw a picture of you looking really big in *Take A Break*, I thought oh no, that's the last thing she needs right now with all that's happening to her.

VANESSA: Well that's why I wanted to get involved in FatFighters –

MARJORIE: (CUTTING HER OFF) Yeah, and then you lost it all again, didn't you?

VANESSA: Yes, but I think I've reached a –

MARJORIE: Yeah, so what are you doing now, going up or down or . . .?

VANESSA: Well I hope I've reached my optimum weight, because I think it's very important when you're dieting to realize actually when that point comes, you know.

MARJORIE: Well I think you could lose another stone, at least. Ok fatties, so it's a Question and Answer with Vanessa Feltz. Now who's got a question for Vanessa? (MEMBERS START TO PUT THEIR HANDS UP) But I will say this, Vanessa will not want to answer questions about the divorce or the time she went a bit loopy loo on that *I'm A*

But I will say this, Vanessa will not want to answer questions about the divorce or the time she went a bit loopy loo on that *I'm A Celebrity Big Brother*, oh and another thing, don't ask her about the whole marriage to Grant Bovey and the thing with the chocolate at her wedding, she's put that behind her.

Celebrity Big Brother, oh and another thing, don't ask her about the whole marriage to Grant Bovey and the thing with the chocolate at her wedding, she's put that behind her.

VANESSA: (LOWERS HER VOICE) That was Anthea Turner.

MARJORIE: Well I don't think you can blame Anthea for that, but anyway, (LOOKS UP FOR THE FIRST QUESTION) Meera? .

VANESSA: Hi, Meera.

MEERA: You must have tried many diets in your time, what was the worst diet you were on?

VANESSA: Well . . .

MARJORIE: Couldn't understand a word, sorry Vanessa, she is Asian, I should have warned you. Question from an English person, yes Pat?

PAT: Hello, Vanessa.

VANESSA: Hi, Pat.

PAT: First off Vanessa, I must say what an inspiration it is to see larger-framed women like yourself on TV.

VANESSA: Thanks, Pat.

PAT: But I wanted to know . . .

MARJORIE: Oh, she's written a bloody essay . . .

PAT: Was it quite a struggle for you to get on TV? It's just, um, I'd love to be a TV presenter, but I feel like my size might hold me back.

VANESSA: Well I think it is hard–

MARJORIE CUTS HER OFF, POINTING AT PAT AND LAUGHING CRUELLY.

MARJORIE: You? On TV? Don't make me laugh, Vanessa may be big but *you* are summin else, I call her Fat Pat, eh Vanessa?

VANESSA: Well actually, Marjorie, I'm putting

together a new show, it's about dieting and our attitudes to food, and I'm looking for some larger people to help present it, so make sure you give me your phone number and I'll be in touch with you after this.

PAT: Oh thanks, I will.

MARJORIE: Oh don't worry Pat, I'll make sure she gets your number. (TURNS TO VANESSA) I could do that, I'd love to be on TV.

VANESSA: No, sorry, not after what I've seen today, you're obviously a total cow. Anybody else?

MARJORIE: Yes, I've got a question for you Vanessa Feltz. (MARJORIE HAWKS UP SOME PHLEGM AND SPITS IN VANESSA'S FACE). Thank you very much, Vanessa Feltz. Vanessa Feltz.

BANK CLERK 1

EXT: THE 'MIDWEST' BANK. WE SEE AN OLD LADY WITH A DOG. SHE BENDS DOWN TO SCOOP SOME DOG POO UP IN A BAG, BUT THEN POPS IT INTO A PASSING OLD LADY'S TARTAN TROLLEY.

TOM V/O: Following the introduction of money to Britain in 1997, banks like this one were opened.

INT: BANK. A VERY BORED LOOKING BANK CLERK, CAROL BEER, IS SITTING AT HER DESK, TALKING TO A CUSTOMER.

CAROL: (DEADPAN) So, how much money do you want to borrow?

CUSTOMER: Two thousand pounds, please.

THE BANK CLERK TURNS TO HER COMPUTER KEYBOARD AND TAPS SOME KEYS.

CAROL: Two – thousand – pounds. (PAUSE). Computer says 'No'.

CUSTOMER: Is there nothing we can do? (THE BANK CLERK SHRUGS, SUPREMELY UNINTERESTED) Right, um, well maybe if I asked to borrow a bit less, I don't know, fifteen hundred pounds?

CAROL TURNS BACK TO HER COMPUTER AND AGAIN TAPS SOME KEYS.

CAROL: Fifteen – hundred – pounds. (PAUSE) Computer says 'No'.

CUSTOMER: Oh, can I have a word with the manager?

CAROL TYPES FOR A FEW SECONDS.

CAROL: (PAUSE) Computer says 'No'.

CUSTOMER: So that's it, there's nothing you can do?

CAROL: Give me a minute. (THE CLERK LEANS CLOSE TO THE COMPUTER AND BEGINS TO WHISPER) There's a man here, says he wants to borrow two thousand pounds (MORE, INAUDIBLE WHISPERING).

FINALLY, CAROL LOOKS UP FROM THE KEYBOARD.

CAROL: Computer says 'No'.

CAROL COUGHS HEAVILY INTO THE CUSTOMER'S FACE.

HARVEY AND JANE — MEET THE PARENTS

EXT: AN EXPENSIVE OLD CAR IS DRIVING UP TO A LARGE HOUSE. HARVEY AND HIS GIRLFRIEND JANE ARE IN THE FRONT SEATS. CELIA AND DAD ARE OUTSIDE THE HOUSE, WAITING TO GREET THEM.

TOM V/O: Posh people are much better and cleverer than common people, and so they live in nicer houses, like this.

GERALD: Oh hello, love's young dream.

What time is dinner, Mummy?

INT: HARVEY'S HOUSE. HARVEY AND JANE ARE ON THE SOFA. CELIA SITS OPPOSITE THEM, WITH GERALD STANDING BEHIND HER.

TOM V/O: Today Harvey Pincher's parents are meeting his girlfriend for the first time.

JANE: It's a lovely house you have here.

GERALD: Yes we're very lucky, it's been in the family for years, but tell us about you, Jane, Harvey says you work in publishing.

JANE: Yes, yes, it's a small House, we mainly do history books.

GERALD: I'll tell you a wonderful battle: battle of Culloden, any books on that?

HARVEY: What time is dinner, Mummy?

CELIA: Oh, it's going to be about another hour.

HARVEY: But I'm hungry.

CELIA: Well you'll have to wait. So how did you two meet?

JANE: It was actually through a friend that I work with who was at Bristol with Harvey . . .

HARVEY: Bitty.

CELIA: No not bitty now, bitty later.

HARVEY: Bitty.

CELIA: Now look, if you have bitty now you're not going to want any supper, are you?

Oh I think it's terribly important to let go.

HARVEY: I want bitty.

CELIA: Come along, then.

HARVEY GETS UP AND GOES OVER TO HIS MUM. HE LIES ACROSS HER LAP AND STARTS TO BREAST-FEED.

CELIA: Come along, then. Sorry Jane, do carry on.

JANE: (VISIBLY SHOCKED) Um . . .

HARVEY CONTINUES TO BREAST-FEED, AS JANE LOOKS ON, HORRIFIED.

CELIA: You were telling us about how you met.

JANE: Oh . . . Well I was at a party and, um, we got talking.

HARVEY BREAKS OFF FROM BREAST-FEEDING TO TURN TO SPEAK TO JANE.

HARVEY: Oh, but I'd seen you once before at Simon's thirtieth, but we didn't really speak then . . .

JANE: No, no, but we sort of (LONG PAUSE) noticed each other.

GERALD: More wine anybody?

HARVEY BREAKS OFF FROM BREAST-FEEDING TO TURN TO SPEAK TO HIS DAD.

HARVEY: Fine thank you, Daddy.

CELIA: Oh you are hungry today, aren't you? So, do you have your own place in London?

JANE: No, no, my brother and I both still live at home with our parents.

CELIA: Really?

JANE: Yes, we have tried to move out but . . . Mum and Dad don't want us to leave.

HARVEY IS STILL BREASTFEEDING WHILE HIS MUM SPEAKS TO JANE.

CELIA: Oh I think it's terribly important to let go.

HARVEY BREAKS OFF AND HIS MUM SLAPS HIM ON THE BACK TO BURP HIM.

HARVEY: (BELCHING LOUDLY) Thank you, Mummy.

GERALD RAISES HIS GLASS TO JANE WHILE HARVEY AND HIS MUM SMILE OVER AT HER. JANE IS STILL IN A STATE OF SHOCK.

GERALD: Welcome to the family.

MR MANN –
DATING AGENCY

INT: DATING AGENCY. ROY IS STANDING BEHIND A DESK. MR MANN ENTERS THE SHOP.

TOM V/O: It's nought o'clock, and at this shop in Phlegm, Mr Mann is looking for a date. I had a date once; it was the eleventh of November.

MR MANN IS STANDING IN FRONT OF ROY'S DESK.

MR MANN: Hello.

ROY: Hello, so how can I help you?

MR MANN: I'm looking to meet a woman with the name of Linda Williams.

(Sidebar text, rotated:)
It's nought o'clock, and at this shop in Phlegm, Mr Mann is looking for a date. I had a date once; it was the eleventh of November.

ROY: Right, so you're looking for a specific person?

MR MANN: No, I'm looking to meet any woman with the name of Linda Williams.

ROY: Any particular reason?

MR MANN: I like that name.

ROY: Right.

MR MANN: It's not my favourite.

ROY: No?

MR MANN: No, my favourite name is Catherine Drew, but at my time of life you can't afford to be too picky. Because as I always say . . .

THERE FOLLOWS A VERY LONG SILENCE.

ROY: Right, ok. (PICKS UP A CLIPBOARD) Let's just take down some of your particulars. What aged woman are you looking to meet?

MR MANN: Oh, really, anybody between the ages of thirty-eight and thirty-nine.

ROY: Right. Height?

MR MANN: She should have some height, yes.

ROY: Hair?

MR MANN: I do prefer it.

ROY: No, any particular length?

MR MANN: Oh anything from here (INDICATING SHOULDER LENGTH WITH HIS HAND) . . . to here.
(HIS HAND DOESN'T MOVE.)

ROY: Right, ok, well I'll just have a look in the file. Oh, I can't see anyone in here, one moment. (GOES TO THE BACK OF THE SHOP AND SHOUTS) Margaret? Margaret?

THERE IS A LONG PAUSE. THE TWO MEN SMILE POLITELY AT EACH OTHER..

MARGARET: (OFF-STAGE) Yes?

Margaret?

ROY: There's a gentlemen here wants to know if we have any women on file by the name of Linda Williams.

MARGARET: Oh, we've got a Lindsey Williams.

ROY: (TURNING TO MR MANN) We've got a Lindsey Williams.

MR MANN: Absolutely no way.

ROY: (SHOUTS) Absolutely no way.

MARGARET: Oh.

ROY: Oh.

MARGARET: There's a Linda Willis.

ROY: Oh yes, there's a Linda Willis.

MR MANN: Would she be interested in changing her name?

ROY: (SHOUTS) Would she be interested in changing her name?

MARGARET: I don't know.

ROY: (TURNING TO MR MANN) She doesn't know.

MR MANN: Oh.

ROY: Oh.

MARGARET: Roy, Roy, have you checked the red file? I think there might be a Linda Williams in there.

ROY LOOKS THROUGH THE FILE ON HIS DESK AND IMMEDIATELY FINDS THE PAGE.

ROY: Oh. Oh yes, how funny, we do have a Linda Williams, yes, she's thirty-eight, she's got shoulder-length hair, very pretty.

MR MANN LOOKS NON-PLUSSED.

MARGARET: Well?

ROY: Well?

MR MANN: (PAUSE) Did I mention she should have a glass eye?

ROY: (SHOUTS) Margaret? Margaret? . . .

EPISODE one

Margaret?

SEBASTIAN AND MICHAEL — PHILIP

EXT: 10 DOWNING STREET. THE PRIME MINISTER GETS OUT OF HIS OFFICIAL CAR WITH VARIOUS MEMBERS OF THE PRESS LOOKING ON AND WALKS UP TO SEBASTIAN, WHO IS WAITING FOR HIM OUTSIDE THE FAMOUS DOOR. SEBASTIAN KISSES THE PRIME MINISTER ON BOTH CHEEKS, HANDS HIM A CUP OF TEA AND GIVES HIS BOTTOM A PROPRIETORIAL PAT AS HE FOLLOWS HIM INSIDE.

TOM V/O: No. 10 Downing Street is the home of the Prime Minister. Of course I was asked to be Prime Minister, but it clashed with a voice over I was doing for Cadbury's Mini Eggs.

INT: 10 DOWNING STREET. THE PRIME MINISTER IS SITTING CASUALLY ON THE EDGE OF HIS DESK, LOOKING THROUGH PAPERS. HIS AIDES, GREGORY AND SEBASTIAN, ARE AWAITING INSTRUCTIONS.

GREGORY: Here are the policy documents for the NATO Summit, Prime Minister.

MICHAEL: Thank you, and I'll need one of you to come with me to Bruges this evening, in advance of the talks tomorrow.

WHILE THE PRIME MINISTER LOOKS THROUGH THE PAPERS, SEBASTIAN PUTS HIS HAND UP LIKE A SCHOOLBOY, DESPERATE TO BE PICKED BY THE TEACHER.

MICHAEL: (LOOKING UP FROM HIS NOTES) Gregory, would you like to go?

GREGORY: I'd be delighted, Prime Minister.

MICHAEL: Would you go and pack my case for me?

GREGORY: (GETTING UP) With pleasure, Prime Minister.

SEBASTIAN: But I know where all your pants and socks are.

MICHAEL: And if you could make sure that the car's standing by, Gregory . . .

GREGORY: Yes, Prime Minister.

GREGORY EXITS.

SEBASTIAN: (PETULANTLY) Yes, Prime Minister, no, Prime Minister, three bags full, Prime Minister.

THE PRIME MINISTER'S INTERCOM BUZZES ON HIS DESK. HE TURNS AND ANSWERS IT.

MICHAEL: Yep?

VOICE ON INTERCOM: The new leader of the opposition is here to see you, Prime Minister.

MICHAEL: Thank you, send him up. (TURNING TO SEBASTIAN) You haven't got a problem with me taking Gregory to the Summit, do you?

SEBASTIAN: No, no, I'm not bothered, no, you guys have fun.

THE PRIME MINISTER GOES TO PUT HIS HAND ON SEBASTIAN'S SHOULDER.

MICHAEL: It's just that I . . .

SEBASTIAN: (IN A HUFF) Don't touch me, please.

THERE IS A KNOCK AT THE DOOR.

MICHAEL: Come in.

THE LEADER OF THE OPPOSITION, PHILIP, ENTERS. HE IS OF COURSE PLAYED BY NIGEL HAVERS.

PHILIP: Oh, so this would be my office. Hi Mike, how are you?

MICHAEL: Don't get too used to it, Phillip. (PHILIP JUMPS WHEN HE REALIZES THAT SEBASTIAN IS STANDING RIGHT BEHIND HIM.) My aide, Sebastian Love.

SEBASTIAN: Hi, just need to search you.

PHILIP: Ok, fine.

Don't worry about him, sister, you want one, you 'ave one.

(SEBASTIAN BEGINS TO SEARCH PHILIP A LITTLE TOO SLOWLY AND EAGERLY, HIS HANDS LINGERING WHEN HE REACHES DOWN TO STROKE PHILIP'S TROUSER-LEGS.)

MICHAEL: Sebastian, I don't think that's necessary . . . Philip, please take a seat.

PHILIP: Oh thank you, very much.

MICHAEL: The Press have been very kind to you today.

PHILIP: Yes, I was pleasantly surprised, even the *Guardian* were pretty positive.

SEBASTIAN: Yeah, gorgeous photo of him wasn't it, Michael? (PUTTING HIS ARM ROUND PHILIP ON THE SOFA) Tea?

PHILIP: I'm sorry?

SEBASTIAN: Cup of tea?

PHILIP: (TO MICHAEL) Are you having one?

SEBASTIAN: Don't worry about him, sister, you want one, you 'ave one.

PHILIP: Well yes, thank you very much.

SEBASTIAN LEAVES WITH HIS NOSE IN THE AIR, SNUBBING THE PRIME MINISTER.

MICHAEL: Are you . . . are you advising your MPs to block the educational reforms I'm putting through?

PHILIP: Oh *that's* the reason you've invited me here.

MICHAEL: I don't think . . .

SEBASTIAN RETURNS AND SITS ON PHILIP'S LAP, HOLDING A PLATE OF CHOCOLATE FINGERS.

SEBASTIAN: Finger?

PHILIP: I'm sorry?

SEBASTIAN: Chocolate finger?

PHILIP: No thanks.

SEBASTIAN: Go on, treat yourself. (WHISPERING SENSUOUSLY TO PHILIP) I like to dunk mine and then suck off the chocolate.

MICHAEL: Sebastian, thank you. (SEBASTIAN GETS UP OFF PHILIP'S LAP) I just don't see that these reforms need to turn into a party political issue.

SEBASTIAN: (BEHIND PHILIP, SUPPORTING HIM) Oh, don't let him bully you.

PHILIP: I think that's a matter between me and the shadow cabinet.

SEBASTIAN: Yeah, you go for it, Girl.

SEBASTIAN BEGINS TO MASSAGE PHILIP'S SHOULDERS WHILE LOOKING DEFIANTLY AT THE PRIME MINISTER.

PHILIP: (GETTING UP TO LEAVE) I'd better be going, I've got an interview with Paxman in a couple of minutes.

MICHAEL: Oh, good luck.

I like to dunk mine and then suck off the chocolate.

SEBASTIAN: (HISSING AT THE PRIME MINISTER) He had you, didn't he?

MICHAEL: He did not.

SEBASTIAN: (MOUTHS) HE DID.

PHILIP AND THE PRIME MINISTER SHAKE HANDS.

PHILIP: Well, it's nice to see you again, Michael, and, er, good luck with the NATO Summit.

MICHAEL: Thank you.

PHILIP: Are you going, Sebastian?

SEBASTIAN: (IN A HUFF) No, he's taking a black boy.

PHILIP: Well, it's nice to meet you.

SEBASTIAN FOLLOWS PHILIP ON HIS WAY OUT.

SEBASTIAN: I'll, um, I'll text you my number, yeah?

PHILIP: Yes, thank you...

SEBASTIAN KISSES PHILIP ON BOTH CHEEKS.

PHILIP: Goodbye.

PHILIP LEAVES.

MICHAEL: Sebastian, that was an extraordinary display.

SEBASTIAN: Ooh, jealous!

SEBASTIAN FLOUNCES OUT AND SLAMS THE DOOR.

MAGGIE AND JUDY – CAKE

EXT: SUMMER FETE. WE SEE A TABLE OF VARIOUS JAMS, SOME OF WHICH HAVE BEEN AWARDED A ROSETTE.

TOM V/O: It's half past Tommy, and Judy and Maggie have completed their judging.

THE VILLAGE VICAR JOINS JUDY AND MAGGIE. HE IS HOLDING A HOMEMADE, ICED CAKE.

VICAR: Ladies, thank you so much for judging the jams.

MAGGIE: It was a pleasure, Vicar.

JUDY: Yes, thank you, Vicar.

VICAR: Care for a fairy cake?

JUDY: Oh, thank you very much.

MAGGIE: Yes, thank you. Mmm, oh, this looks lovely . . . (TAKES A BITE) Mmm, delicious.

VICAR: These were actually made by the people in the homeless shelter.

MAGGIE VOMITS ALL OVER THE VICAR'S FACE AND INTO HER OWN TEACUP FOR SEVERAL SECONDS. WHEN SHE HAS STOPPED, SHE TAKES A DELICATE SIP FROM THE CUP.

LOU AND ANDY – FEEDING THE DUCKS

EXT: PARK. LOU IS PUSHING ANDY ALONG IN HIS WHEELCHAIR, BY A LAKE.

TOM V/O: After a morning spent removing all the Ks from Andy's Alphabetti

Spaghetti, Lou is taking his friend to the park.

LOU AND ANDY STOP TO FEED THE DUCKS. WE NOTICE A GROUP OF YOUNG LADS IN THE BACKGROUND WHO TAKE AN INTEREST IN THE NEW ARRIVALS.

LOU: Oh, don't eat all the bread, that's for the ducks.

ANDY: Yeah, I know.

THE GROUP OF LADS START TO CALL ANDY NAMES.

LAD: Oi! Oi, Ironside.

ANDY: Come over here and say that.

LOU: Rise above it.

ANDY: They're taking the mick

LOU: Well just ignore it.

ONE LAD THROWS A CAN, WHICH HITS LOU ON THE SHOULDER.

ANDY: Some one should give them lot a smack.

LOU: But I thought you said you were against violence. I thought you said that violence is the last bastion of moral cowardice.

ANDY: Yeah, I know.

LOU: Well leave it, then. Come on, let's feed the ducks.

LAD: Oi! Oi Davros!

LOU HAS TURNED AWAY TO LOOK PEACEFULLY OUT AT THE LAKE WHILE HE THROWS BREAD TO THE DUCKS.

LOU: Ah, peaceful here innit?

– IN THE BACKGROUND WE SEE ANDY GET UP AND RUN OVER TO THE LADS AND BEAT THEM UP, WHILE LOU TALKS TO HIMSELF, WISTFULLY.

LOU: That's why I like it, a chance to really think and reflect on your life. I find the water very calming and I know you do too, especially on a

I thought you said you were against violence. I thought you said that violence is the last bastion of moral cowardice.

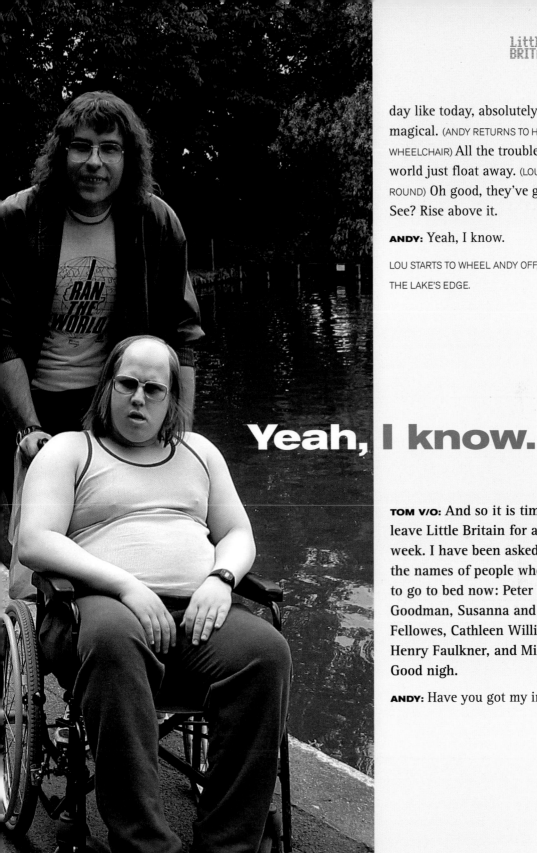

day like today, absolutely magical. (ANDY RETURNS TO HIS WHEELCHAIR) All the troubles of the world just float away. (LOU TURNS ROUND) Oh good, they've gone. See? Rise above it.

ANDY: Yeah, I know.

LOU STARTS TO WHEEL ANDY OFF, AROUND THE LAKE'S EDGE.

Yeah, I know.

TOM V/O: And so it is time to leave Little Britain for another week. I have been asked to read the names of people who have to go to bed now: Peter Goodman, Susanna and Robin Fellowes, Cathleen Willis, Sir Henry Faulkner, and Mickey, Good nigh.

ANDY: Have you got my inhaler?

EPISODE
one

EPISODE *two*

TOM V/O: Britain, Britain, Britain, what an absolutely terrific place to live. We have no crime here, and why? It's not because we hang, draw and quarter people for parking violations or disembowel litter louts, no, it's because of the people of Britain, they are the bestest, goodliest people on God's fair earth. And it is these everyday folksters that we look at for a bit today. Keep it real.

EMILY AND FLORENCE – WEDDING DRESS

EXT: DRESS SHOP. EMILY AND FLORENCE ARE ON A TANDEM CYCLING TOWARDS THE SHOP, GREETING PASSERS-BY AS THEY GO. THEY PARK THE BIKE OUTSIDE THE SHOP AND ENTER.

TOM V/O: Emily and Florence are transvestites. Some people are intolerant of transvestism, but live and let live I say, everyone is equal and deserves the same rights. Apart from lezzers.

INT: DRESS SHOP.

EMILY: Now, let me do the talking. (LOOKING THROUGH A RAIL OF DRESSES) Oh aren't these ladies' dresses delightful, my lady friend?

FLORENCE: Yes Emily, oh this one's very you, I think.

A SHOP ASSISTANT COMES OVER TO OFFER ASSISTANCE, BUT GASPS WHEN EMILY AND FLORENCE TURN ROUND.

SHOP ASSISTANT: Hello, can I help you ladies? Oh!

EMILY: Hello, yes, I'm getting married and I would like to purchase a dress, please.

SHOP ASSISTANT: F–for your fiancée?

EMILY: No, for me, I am a lady. (FLORENCE WHISPERS SOMETHING TO EMILY) Oh yes, and we require a bridesmaid's dress for my young lady friend here, Florence.

FLORENCE: Yes, I'm ever so excited, I've never been a bridesmaid before. I'm only fifteen, you see.

SHOP ASSISTANT: Right, what sort of dress are you looking for?

EMILY: Oh a ladies' dress that ladies wear, white of course with frilly bits and . . . shit. This one is very nice.

SHOP ASSISTANT: Excuse me. (SHOUTS TO THE BACK OF THE SHOP) Elizabeth!

ELIZABETH: (OFF STAGE) Yes?

SHOP ASSISTANT: Have we got any of the Marie Antoinettes?

ELIZABETH: What size?

SHOP ASSISTANT: Um, one to fit a man. (TURNING TO LOOK AT EMILY AGAIN) A large man.

ELIZABETH: I don't think so, I'll have a look in the stock room.

SHOP ASSISTANT: Ok.

FLORENCE COUGHS TO REMIND HER THAT SHE ALSO WANTS A DRESS.

SHOP ASSISTANT: (SHOUTING) Oh, and bridesmaid's outfits; for a short fat bloke; with a moustache.

Oh, and bridesmaid's outfits; for a short fat bloke; with a moustache.

FLORENCE LOOKS OVER HER SHOULDER, INNOCENTLY, FOR A MAN FITTING THIS DESCRIPTION.

WE CUT TO A SHOT OF THE CURTAIN OF A CHANGING ROOM. EMILY IS CLEARLY STRUGGLING TO GET INTO HER DRESS.

EMILY: (GIRLISH FRUSTRATION) Oh, eh, oh, oh . . . (ANGRY MAN'S VOICE) get this *bloody* thing on.

FLORENCE IS SITTING ON A CHAIR WAITING, FLANKED BY THE TWO SHOP ASSISTANTS.

FLORENCE: Ladies' noises.

EMILY OPENS THE CHANGING-ROOM CURTAIN AND WALKS OUT TRIUMPHANTLY, WEARING A WEDDING DRESS.

FLORENCE: Oh Emily, you look simply divine.

EMILY: This man I'm marrying will be so pleased.

SHOP ASSISTANT: How's the fit?

EMILY: It's perfect. I'm normally an eight and this is a ten, so.

SHOP ASSISTANT: Well, if you're sure.

EMILY: I'm quite sure, I'll just go and pop my clothes back on.

EMILY TURNS ROUND TO REVEAL HER BARE BACK AND HAIRY BOTTOM THROUGH THE OPEN ZIP AS SHE BENDS DOWN.

FLORENCE: (TO THE ASSISTANTS) Pretty as a peach.

SEBASTIAN AND MICHAEL – THE PRESIDENT

EXT: 10 DOWNING STREET. SEBASTIAN AND THE PRIME MINISTER GET OUT OF THE OFFICIAL CAR. WHILE THE PRIME MINISTER HEADS FOR THE DOOR, SEBASTIAN POSES FOR PHOTOGRAPHS, LEANING BACK FLIRTATIOUSLY ON THE BONNET OF THE CAR.

TOM V/O: Britain is a democracy where any citizen can become Prime Minister, as long as they've got a degree and aren't black. Today the Prime Minister is having a very important Summit with the American President.

INT: 10 DOWNING STREET, THE PRIME MINISTER'S OFFICE. THE PRIME MINISTER SITS FACING THE AMERICAN PRESIDENT ACROSS A DESK. SEBASTIAN AND MARVIN, THE PRESIDENT'S PERSONAL AIDE, STAND BEHIND THEIR RESPECTIVE LEADERS

MICHAEL: I hear what you say but I think what you're proposing is an abuse of our friendship.

SEBASTIAN PULLS A TRIUMPHANT FACE AT MARVIN, OVER THE PRIME MINISTER'S HEAD.

AMERICAN PRESIDENT: Look, there are no half measures, either you are with the United States on this or you are against us.

MARVIN RESPONDS BY MAKING AN 'L' FOR 'LOSER' SIGN ON HIS FOREHEAD AT SEBASTIAN.

MICHAEL: Well, I think we'll have to take advice from the United Nations, because I refuse to be bullied into making a snap decision.

SEBASTIAN LICKS HIS FINGER AND CHALKS UP AN IMAGINARY POINT IN THE AIR AT MARVIN.

AMERICAN PRESIDENT: United Nations can go to hell. If you want this special relationship with our country to continue, you're going to have to start delivering.

MARVIN MOONWALKS.

MICHAEL: Before you rush in to anything, perhaps you'd like to see what the British Intelligence has to say.

SEBASTIAN PULLS A CHILDISH FACE AT MARVIN.

AMERICAN PRESIDENT: And perhaps you'd like to see what the CIA has gathered.

MARVIN WINDS HIS FINGER UP AND DOWN AT SEBASTIAN.

MICHAEL: Sebastian, could you get the document for the President, please?

SEBASTIAN: Yes, Prime Minister, I'll get it right now, Prime Minister.

AMERICAN PRESIDENT: Er, Marvin, can you get the CIA files for the Prime Minister, please?

MARVIN: (SALUTING TWICE) Yes sir, Mr President sir!

MARVIN SALUTES BEFORE MARCHING OVER TO JOIN SEBASTIAN BY THE LEATHER SOFAS.

SEBASTIAN: My Prime Minister's so much better than your President.

MARVIN: Mr President's big and powerful and so rugged, your Prime Minister sucks.

SEBASTIAN: How dare you.

SEBASTIAN AND MARVIN START SLAPPING EACH OTHER.

MARVIN: Get your hands off me please, sir.

SEBASTIAN: Get your hands off me.

MARVIN: Get your hands off me.

SEBASTIAN: You will, you will.

MICHAEL: (STERNLY) What on earth is going on?

SEBASTIAN & MARVIN: (SHOUTING OVER EACH OTHER UNINTELLIGIBLY)

MICHAEL: Enough.

SEBASTIAN & MARVIN: (MORE UNINTELLIGIBLE SQUABBLING)

THE PRIME MINISTER AND THE PRESIDENT APPROACH THE PAIR. SEBASTIAN AND MARVIN KEEP LOOKING DOWN, LIKE NAUGHTY SCHOOLBOYS.

MICHAEL: Enough. Mr President, we have to go to the photo call. This behaviour is completely inappropriate, this is a difficult enough situation, now you're making it a lot worse.

AMERICAN PRESIDENT: Let me handle this. You two should be ashamed of yourselves. Two senior aides acting like a pair of third graders. You're an embarrassment.

THE PRIME MINISTER AND PRESIDENT LEAVE THE ROOM.

SEBASTIAN & MARVIN: ('HANDBAGS' VOICE) Oooh!

My Prime Minister's so much better than your President.

BUBBLES DEVERE – SUN BED

EXT: HILL GRANGE HEALTH SPA. BUBBLES IS SITTING IN HER GOWN IN THE GARDENS, READING A MAGAZINE.

TOM V/O: Mrs DeVere has been staying at Hill Grange Health Spa for five months now. And has so far lost nearly an ounce.

MR HUTTON, THE MANAGER, COMES OUT OF THE SPA AND SHOUTS OVER TO BUBBLES.

MR HUTTON: Mrs DeVere, I need to speak to you about this unpaid bill. Mrs DeVere!

BUBBLES GETS UP HURRIEDLY FROM THE LOUNGER AND RUNS AWAY. AS SHE GOES,
THE BELT OF HER GOWN CATCHES ON THE CHAIR, PULLING THE GOWN OFF.

WE SEE BUBBLES RUNNING NAKED PAST THE SWIMMING POOL, SAYING HELLO TO PEOPLE AS SHE GOES.

BUBBLES: Hello Baz, hello Mrs Papadopoulos!

MR HUTTON FOLLOWS.

MR HUTTON: Mrs DeVere!

BUBBLES ENTERS A TREATMENT ROOM.

BUBBLES: My turn now darling, quick, quick, off.

BUBBLES PULLS A WOMAN OFF THE SUN BED AND QUICKLY LIES DOWN
UNDER THE LAMP. MR HUTTON ENTERS THE ROOM TO FIND BUBBLES
HIDDEN BENEATH THE LID OF THE SOLARIUM.

MR HUTTON: Mrs DeVere.

BUBBLES: Call me Bubbles.

MR HUTTON: Can I have a word?

BUBBLES: Can't you see I'm on the solaribed, darling?

MR HUTTON: Mrs DeVere, I need to resolve this payment situation.
You owe us nearly twenty thousand pounds now.

BUBBLES: I will discuss this with you as soon as I'm done, darling.

THE SHOT FADES TO BLACK AND FADES BACK IN AGAIN. MR HUTTON IS STILL WAITING, LOOKING AT HIS WATCH.

MR HUTTON: Mrs DeVere, you've been under there for over three hours now.

BUBBLES: Yes alright, darling.

(MR HUTTON LIFTS UP THE LID OF THE SUN BED, TO REVEAL BUBBLES, CHARRED BLACK AND WITH SMOKE COMING OFF HER.
SHE CAREFULLY TAKES HER GOGGLES OFF TO REVEAL TWO TINY, UNBURNT WHITE PATCHES AROUND HER EYES)

BUBBLES: (DEADPAN) Will you excuse me for a moment please, Mr Hutton? I'm a little bit on fire.

SHE WALKS OFF, LEAVING MR HUTTON STUNNED.

> Yes alright, darling. Will you excuse me for a moment please, Mr Hutton? I'm a little bit on fire.

LOU AND ANDY — ANYA

EXT: PUB. LOU IS PUSHING ANDY ALONG THE STREET. –AS THEY PASS A WOMAN WHO IS TALKING INTO HER MOBILE PHONE, ANDY TRIES TO GRAB HER HANDBAG. LOU APOLOGISES TO THE WOMAN AND CHIDES ANDY.

TOM V/O: Today Lou is taking his friend Andy to a local pub.

INT: LOU AND ANDY SITTING AT A TABLE INSIDE THE PUB.

LOU: (PRIMPING HIS HAIR EXCITEDLY) Do I look alright? Andy?

ANDY: Yeah.

LOU: Now, you know I've been seeing a lot more of Anya recently, since she got her visa through, so I want you two to get to know each other, alright?

ANDY: Yeah, I know.

LOU SPOTS ANYA ENTERING THE PUB, AND STANDS UP TO MEET HER.

LOU: (LAUGHING NERVOUSLY) Oh, here she is!

ANYA HAS A STRONG EASTERN-EUROPEAN ACCENT.

ANYA: Hello, Lou.

LOU: Hello, Anya, may I say you are looking lovely.

LOU KISSES ANYA, AWKWARDLY.

ANYA: Oh.

LOU: Here we are. Now, this is Anya, who I was telling you about.

ANYA: Hello, I'm Anya.

LOU: Yeah, I know.

ANDY: Take a seat. Now, um, let me get everybody a drink, Anya, what would you like?

Hello, Anya, may I say you are looking lovely.

Hello, Lou.

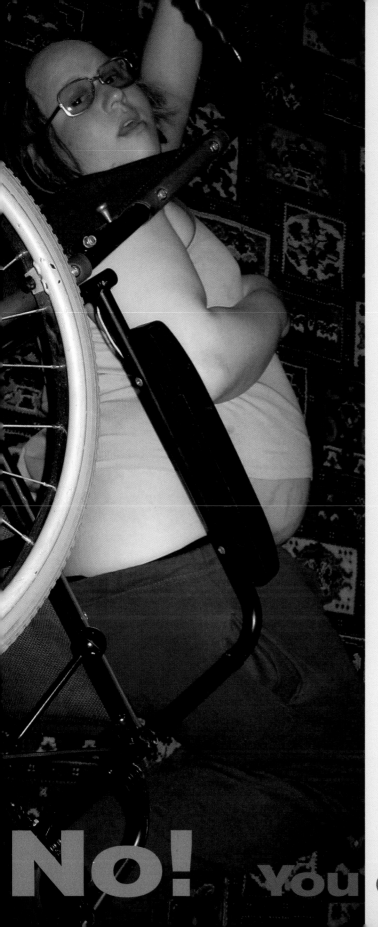

ANYA: Oh, um, a pint of bitter, please.

LOU: (CLEARLY BESOTTED WITH ANYA) 'Pint of bitter, please.' And Andy?

ANDY: Don't want nothing.

LOU: (QUIETLY) Now don't be silly, what do you want?

ANDY: Pint, and another one.

LOU: Ok, won't be a mo'.

LOU BLOWS A KISS TO ANYA AS HE WALKS OVER TO THE BAR.

ANYA: So Andy, er, Lou tells me a lot about you. He's a very nice man, isn't he? I like him very much.

ANDY STANDS UP, PUTS HIS WHEELCHAIR CAREFULLY AND DELIBERATELY ON ITS SIDE, SPINS THE WHEEL AND THEN LIES ON THE FLOOR.

LOU BRINGS THE DRINKS OVER TO THE TABLE AND SEES ANDY ON THE FLOOR.

LOU: Oh my goodness! What happened?

ANDY: She pushed me.

LOU: No! (SNARLING MALEVOLENTLY AT ANYA) You evil Pole.

EPISODE TWO

No! You evil Pole.

UNIVERSITY OFFICE 1

EXT: SIGN FOR 'UNIVERSITY OF THE NORTH WEST MIDLANDS'.

TOM V/O: Being at university is a very harsh basket, with students having to attend anything up to one lecture a term.

INT: UNIVERSITY OFFICE. LINDA SITS AT HER DESK, TALKING TO A LARGE, SHORT-HAIRED YOUNG LADY.

JOANNA: I'm sure I can get it finished by the end of the week.

LINDA: And when's it due in?

JOANNA: Today.

LINDA: Oh, I'll ring Martin and see. Hello Martin, it's Linda . . . yep, I've got a student here needs an extension on her feminist poetry essay. It's Joanna Harding. Jo Harding. Um, how can I describe her? Quite short hair, a few piercings . . . wears a lot of black . . . combat trousers . . . That's right, the big fat lesbian, yeah.

LINDA PUTS THE PHONE DOWN AND TURNS TO JOANNA.

LINDA: Friday will be fine.

DR LAWRENCE AND ANNE – BOWLING ALLEY

INT: BOWLING ALLEY. DR LAWRENCE AND DR BEAGRIE ARE WALKING OVER TOWARDS THE RECEPTION DESK.

TOM V/O: Meanwhile, in Little Bentcock, Dr Lawrence is showing Dr Beagrie how one of his patients, Anne, is getting on in her new job.

DR LAWRENCE: Of an evening when it's still light, we encourage Anne to leave the hospital and work here. Watch this.

ANNE IS STANDING BEHIND THE RECEPTION DESK, CHATTING ON THE PHONE IN A NORMAL VOICE AS THE TWO MEN ARRIVE.

ANNE: No, it's very, very quiet today. (NOTICING THE DOCTORS) Call you back later.

DR LAWRENCE: Hello, Anne.

ANNE: (SQUAWKING) Eh eh eh!

DR LAWRENCE: Can I have a pair of size nine bowling shoes, please?

Eh eh eh!

DR LAWRENCE PUTS HIS OWN SHOES ON THE COUNTER. ANNE TAKES HIS SHOES, RUBS THEM OVER HER BREASTS AND CROTCH AND PASSES HIM A PAIR OF RED STILETTOS IN EXCHANGE.

ANNE: Eh eh eh!

DR LAWRENCE: No, size nine *bowling* shoes please, Anne.

ANNE: Eh eh eh!

ANNE SLAMS DOWN A PAIR OF BOWLING SHOES ONTO THE COUNTER.

DR LAWRENCE TAKES THE SHOES AND THEY GO TO LEAVE.

DR LAWRENCE: Thank you very much, Anne, see you later.

ANNE STOPS AN ASTONISHED DR BEAGRIE, HANDS HIM A WAD OF MONEY FROM THE TILL AND STROKES HIS FACE.

MARJORIE DAWES/FATFIGHTERS – PAT AND PAUL

INT: FATFIGHTERS CLUB. THE FATFIGHTERS ARE SITTING DOWN READY FOR THE MEETING TO BEGIN. ONE OF THE MEMBERS, TANIA, GETS UP TO BE WEIGHED.

TOM V/O: FatFighters is a very valuable organisation which offers help and support to those who are serious about losing weight. Like these fat bastards.

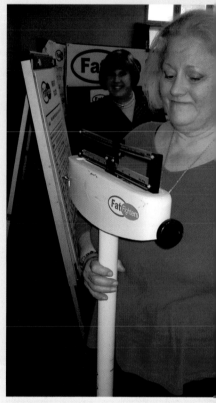

TANIA: (ON THE SCALES) Nineteen stone five.

MARJORIE: Oh no, you've put on again, haven't you? Oh dear, it's not easy is it?

TANIA: No.

MARJORIE: You see your problem is, Tania, you're fat *and* old. It gets harder, and there's no man is there, you're on your own.

TANIA: Yes, my husband left me.

MARJORIE: Yeah, well he would have done. Yeah, younger woman weren't it?

TANIA: Yeah.

MARJORIE: Forty-nine, yeah, so you're on your own now, every night crying and eating. Well, at least you've got all of us here at FatFighters to make you feel better. Off you pop. (TO HERSELF, BUT LOUD ENOUGH FOR ALL TO HEAR) Oh, she stinks an' all. Pat, you're next. Pat, Fat Pat, fatty, Patty boom boom.

PAT STANDS ON THE SCALES.

PAT: Seventeen stone two.

MARJORIE: Oh no, you've gone up an' all, two pound.

PAT: I was doing so well.

PAUL: (CHUCKLES) Don't matter, I like something to hold on to.

GENTLE LAUGHTER FROM THE OTHER FATFIGHTERS.

MARJORIE: Sorry, what was that?

PAT: He was just making a joke. We've sort of started seeing each other.

MARJORIE: (HIGH-PITCHED DISGUST) Urgh! Urgh, how long's this been going on?

PAUL: Couple of weeks.

MARJORIE: Couple of weeks? Urgh!. Mind you, in a way I suppose it does make sense, two fatties together. Yeahj, you do often get that, fat on fat.

MEERA: Maybe we shall have our first FatFighters wedding.

MARJORIE: Oh, in English please if you are going to say anything, Meera. How does the mechanics of your love making work, do you have to use a winch or do you have a system of weights and pulleys, or?

PAUL: What kind of question's that?

MARJORIE: In fact no, I don't want to know, but I will say this, when you do get two fatties together, or fat love (MARJORIE WRITES 'FAT LOVE' ON THE WIPE BOARD)– they often do pile it on, do you see what I'm saying? Because there's no incentive, do you see what I'm saying, because they're both fat.

PAUL: Yeah, well I think she's lovely.

MARJORIE: Mm, yeah, that's not helping her. I've said it before, and I'll say it again, Pat is morbidly obese. In fact I've only ever seen one person fatter than Pat and that was Babar Papa. In a way the kindest thing you can do is chuck her and tell her to give you a call when she's lost a few stone.

PAT: (DEJECTED) Thanks, Marjorie.

MARJORIE: That's no problem, Pat, I'm only thinking of you, because I really care about you, because you are now, really, an enormous fat pig. Paul, you're next.

DAFFYD — VILLAGE FETE

EXT: VILLAGE FETE. DAFFYD IS SITTING ALONE AT THE 'GAY & LESBIAN STALL'.

TOM V/O: Over in Llandewi Breffi, devoted homosexualist Daffyd Thomas is taking part in the village fete.

A LITTLE OLD LADY, MRS WILLIAMS, WALKS OVER TO DAFFYD'S STALL.

That's no problem, Pat, I'm only thinking of you, because I really care about you, because you are now, really, an enormous fat pig.

I wonder what the church would make of my gay and lesbian stall. Well I'm not moving I tell you, I'm here, I'm queer, get used to it.

MRS WILLIAMS: Hello, Daffyd.

DAFFYD: Good afternoon.

MRS WILLIAMS: Ooh, how much are your poppers?

DAFFYD: This is a gay stall, for gays only.

MRS WILLIAMS: My grandson's gay.

DAFFYD: Yes, it's probably just a phase.

THE LOCAL VICAR WALKS OVER AND SHAKES MRS WILLIAMS'S HAND.

VICAR: Hello Mrs Williams, lovely flowers in the church last Sunday, thank you for those.

MRS WILLIAMS: My pleasure, Vicar. Oh, have you met Daffyd?

VICAR: Ah no, I don't think I have.

DAFFYD: Daffyd Thomas, the only gay in the village.

VICAR: Hello, I'm Glyn, I'm the new vicar.

DAFFYD: I wonder what the church would make of my gay and lesbian stall. Well I'm not moving I tell you, I'm here, I'm queer, get used to it.

VICAR: No, no, no, I think it's wonderful that you're here, one thing I really want to do is bring more gay people from the village into the church.

DAFFYD: Gay *person*.

EPISODE TWO

MRS WILLIAMS: Do these butt plugs come with batteries?

DAFFYD: Put that down!

A CAMP VERGER IN A TIGHT PVC OUTFIT WALKS OVER.

VERGER: Oh, a gay stall, isn't that lovely, darling? (THEY KISS) Hello, I'm the verger.

HE OFFERS HIS HAND TO DAFFYD.

DAFFYD: What the hell was that?

VICAR: Oh we're a couple, we met at my last parish, in Merthyr Tydfil.

DAFFYD: And you had to come here, I don't know why I bother.

VICAR: Well I think it's a cause for celebration, I mean you're gay, we're gay.

DAFFYD: Well I shall be writing to the Bishop.

Do these butt plugs come with batteries?

VICAR: Oh I wouldn't bother, he's gay.

VERGER: Actually he's bi.

DAFFYD: What ever happened to good old-fashioned religious homophobia?

VERGER: Oh it's all change, dear. (PICKS UP A DILDO FROM THE TABLE) Oh, now this would be very nice for the archdeacon.

VICAR: Oh yes, have you got one in black?

DAFFYD: That's disgusting. (SLAMMING THE DILDO BACK ON THE TABLE) Right, I'm off.

VICAR: Where are you going?

DAFFYD: Well I can't stay here now, can I?

VICAR: What's the matter?

DAFFYD: I'm the only gay in this village.

DAFFYD STORMS OFF.

MRS WILLIAMS: I've said it before vicar, and I'll say it again. What that boy needs is a nice big cock up his arse.

UNIVERSITY OFFICE 2

INT: UNIVERSITY OFFICE. LINDA IS SITTING AT HER DESK TALKING TO KENNETH, A YOUNG, MALE CHINESE STUDENT.

KENNETH: If you could ask I'd really appreciate it.

LINDA: Ok, I'll see what I can do... Martin, it's Linda, I've got a student here who needs the rest of the week off . . . personal reasons . . . mum's ill. Yeah, it's Kenneth Lough. Um, how can I describe him? He's got straight black hair . . . yellowish skin . . . *slight* smell of soya sauce. That's it, the ching chong Chinaman. Ok. (TO KENNETH) He says that's fine.

KENNETH IS SHOCKED.

He's got straight black hair . . .
yellowish skin . . . *slight* smell of
soya sauce.

Not bitty now,

HARVEY AND JANE — RESTAURANT

EXT: RESTAURANT. A SIGN IN THE WINDOW READS 'ALL YOU CAN EAT £5000'.

TOM V/O: At this restaurant in Harlot, Harvey and Jane's parents are meeting each other for the first time.

INT: RESTAURANT. GERALD IS MAKING A TOAST. HARVEY, CELIA, JANE AND JANE'S PARENTS ARE ALL SITTING AROUND THE TABLE.

GERALD: . . . join me in raising a toast for Harvey and Jane.

JANE'S MUM & DAD: Harvey and Jane!

HARVEY: (CLINKING GLASSES) To us.

CELIA: We've certainly got our work cut out for September, haven't we?

bitty later.

GERALD: Yes, do you want me to see if the golf club's free for the reception?

JANE'S DAD: Thank you, that would be great.

HARVEY: (TO HIS MUM) Still hungry.

CELIA: Well have something when you get back, yes?

HARVEY: Hungry.

CELIA: When our eldest daughter got married, she decided she wanted to have it in a very small village church, didn't she, Harvey?

HARVEY: Bitty.

CELIA: No, darling. The problem was that the church only held a hundred, and she wanted –

HARVEY: Bitty.

CELIA: Not bitty now, bitty later.

JANE: Mum's drawn up a list of some people she'd like to invite.

JANE'S MUM: Yes, we've got some family in New Zealand.

HARVEY: Bitty.

CELIA: Darling, you've just had pudding.

HARVEY: Bitty, bitty.

CELIA: Excuse me.

HARVEY LIES DOWN ON HIS MUM'S LAP, SHE LIFTS HER TOP AND HE BEGINS TO BREAST-FEED. JANE AND HER PARENTS LOOK ON, STUNNED.

CELIA: (LOOKING UP, BRIGHTLY) You were saying . . .?

JANE'S MUM: (IN SHOCK) We were just saying that . . . we can do that list.

WAITER: Coffee . . .

GERALD: Oh, lovely. Are you having coffee, son?

HARVEY: (LOOKING UP FROM HIS FEED) No thank you, Daddy, I'm fine with milk.

GERALD BEGINS TO POUR HIMSELF SOME MILK FROM THE JUG.

GERALD: Hard isn't it? All these relatives you see once a year, bloody bores, and you feel you have to invite them. (NOTICING THAT THE MILK HAS RUN OUT) Oh, they never do bring enough.

HARVEY: Let me.

HARVEY HOLDS THE LITTLE JUG UNDER ONE OF HIS MUM'S BREASTS. SHE TRIES TO GUIDE SOME MILK INTO THE JUG, BUT ENDS UP SPRAYING MILK ALL OVER JANE'S MUM.

HARVEY: Sorry.

HARVEY PASSES THE REFILLED JUG TO HIS DAD, WHO TOPS UP HIS CUP.

HARVEY: There.

GERALD: Oh lovely. (TO JANE'S SHOCKED FATHER) So, do you follow the cricket?

BANK CLERK 2

EXT: THE 'MIDWEST' BANK. WE SEE AN OLD LADY DUTIFULLY USING A TRANSPARENT PLASTIC BAG TO PICK UP SOME DOG POO FROM THE PAVEMENT. SHE STANDS UP, AND POPS IT STRAIGHT INTO A NEARBY RED POST BOX.

TOM V/O: Banks in Britain are extremely popular, in fact there's nothing I like more than a jolly good bank.

INT: BANK OFFICE. BANK CLERK CAROL BEER IS SITTING AT HER COMPUTER, TYPING AWAY. ACROSS THE DESK, A MOTHER AND HER YOUNG SON WAIT EXPECTANTLY.

CAROL: So how old is he?

CUSTOMER: Go on, tell the nice lady.

BOY: Nearly six.

CAROL: (TYPING) Nearly – six.

CUSTOMER: He's just got some money from his uncle and he wants to open his first bank account.

CAROL HANDS OVER A LEAFLET AND A BRIGHTLY COLOURED, NEW PIGGY BANK.

CAROL: Well, we do have a junior saver account. (GLARING MENACINGLY AT THE BOY) Right, you get a free Percy piggy bank, oink, oink.

CUSTOMER: (BRIGHTLY) Oh, lovely.

CAROL: And you get entered into a prize draw to win a free trip to Euro Disney.

CUSTOMER: (TO HER SON, EXCITEDLY) Oh, I think he'd like to open one of these please, won't you?

(CAROL TAPS AWAY AT THE KEYBOARD AND PAUSES BEFORE LOOKING UP.)

CAROL: Computer says 'No'.

CAROL REACHES ACROSS THE DESK, GRABS BACK THE PIGGY BANK FROM THE CRESTFALLEN BOY – AND THEN COUGHS ON HIM, HEAVILY.

Well, we do have a junior saver account. Right, you get a free Percy piggy bank, oink, oink.

Oh, I think he'd like to open one of these please, won't you?

Computer says 'No'.

EPISODE two

VICKY POLLARD – PARK

EXT: FLATS. TWO TEENAGERS, KARL AND BETHANY, ARE SITTING TOGETHER ON A BENCH, TALKING. WE SEE VICKY, WEARING ONLY A BRIGHT PINK BIKINI, CLUMSILY ROLLER-BLADE OVER TO THE COUPLE.

TOM V/O: It's a school day, so Vicky Pollard has taken herself off to the park.

VICKY: Hi, Karl.

KARL: Hi, um . . .?

VICKY: Vicky. (TO BETHANY) Move, actually. (VICKY CLEARS A SPACE BETWEEN THEM AND SITS DOWN) So, er, you going down Kelly's party later?

KARL: Might do.

VICKY: If you want I'll go with you yeah?

KARL: If I go, I'll go with Bethany.

BETHANY: Er, Vicky, why are you always trying to get off with my boyfriends?

VICKY: Oh my god I so can't believe you just said that. This is like the time I threw Anita's Nokia in the canal as a joke and she's like you have well got to buy me another one and I'm like get over it and then Paul Rowley came over who's adopted anyway and started stirring it all up started saying that I fancy Mark Bennett. But oh my God just because I have sex with someone doesn't mean I fancy them. But everyone knows you've been gert jealous of me because I saw Christina Aguilera on the bus.

BETHANY: You never saw her.

VICKY: I did, she got off at Fishponds.

**ButohmyGodjustbecause
Ihavesexwithsomeonedoesn't
meanIfancythem.**

Uhh, don't be disgusting, why would I fancy him? Er minging, he's well gay anyway.

BETHANY: You're such a liar, anyway stop trying to get off with my boyfriend.

VICKY: Uhh, don't be disgusting, why would I fancy him? Er minging, he's well gay anyway.

BETHANY: Well Rochelle said you told her you well fancy him, did you?

VICKY: No but yeah but no but yeah but no I don't actually and Rochelle is well going to get beatings now for saying that. God she's such a liar what about the time she didn't go to Sunita's house because she said her dad was really ill and it turned out all he had was a brain haemorrhage. Anyway Karl does really fancy me because he passed me a note during metalwork saying he wanted to take me round the back of the language lab to touch my Forest of Dean.

KARL: Piss off.

VICKY TRIES TO GET UP FROM THE BENCH, BUT IS CLEARLY HAVING TROUBLE BALANCING ON THE ROLLER-BLADES.

VICKY: Don't worry, I was going anyway you pair of total lesbo spackers and if I see either of you again you're both dead! (PAUSE) Can you give me a hand up, please. Thanks. I'm more confident on the road.

DENNIS WATERMAN – CAPTAIN BIRDSEYE

INT: JEREMY RENT'S OFFICE.

TOM V/O: Jeremy Rent is an actor's agent. I haven't heard from my agent for many years, but then she is hopelessly dead.

JEREMY IS SITTING AT HIS DESK, IN THE MIDDLE OF A PHONE CALL.

JEREMY: So that's a confirmed booking for my client Melvin Hayes to appear as Buttons in *Cinderella* at the Harlequin Theatre, Red Hill, this Christmas. Oh yes, the fee. Um, how does two hundred pounds a week sound? (PAUSE) Well I'm sorry, but I can't afford to pay you any more, goodbye.

WE HEAR A FLY BUZZING. JEREMY ATTEMPTS TO WAVE IT AWAY.

VOICE ON PHONE INTERCOM: Dennis Waterman here to see you.

JEREMY: Lovely, send him in.

TINY DENNIS WATERMAN ENTERS THE ROOM.

DENNIS: Hello.

JEREMY: Hello, Den.

DENNIS: Hot today, isn't it?

JEREMY: Oh yes, it's sweltering.

DENNIS: I brought you a can of pop.

JEREMY: Oh, that's very kind of you. Do you need a hand bringing it in?

DENNIS: Oh no, I'll be fine.

JEREMY CONTINUES TO BAT AT THE BUZZING FLY. TINY DENNIS ENTERS, BALANCING ON AN ENORMOUS, ROLLING CAN OF COLA. WITH MUCH EFFORT, HE SUCCEEDS IN LIFTING IT OVER HIS HEAD AND PASSING IT TO JEREMY.

DENNIS: Ohhh.

WE CUT BACK TO JEREMY, WHO REACHES OUT AND TAKES A TINY CAN OF COLA.

JEREMY: Thank you very much. (TAKING A DRINK) Oh lovely, thank you. Now, I've had a call from the people at Birds Eye.

MORE BUZZING.

DENNIS: Is there a fly in here?

JEREMY: Yes, don't worry, it won't hurt you.

SUDDENLY, A GIANT FLY APPEARS AND CIRCLES A VERY FRIGHTENED DENNIS.

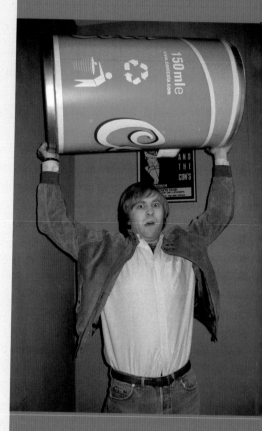

I brought you a can of pop.

Oh, that's very kind of you. Do you need a hand bringing it in?

DENNIS: Ah, ah, ah, ah!

JEREMY: Just ignore it, it will fly away. (IT DOES SO) Anyway they're making some new adverts, and they want you to be Captain Birdseye.

DENNIS: So they want me to star in it, write the feem toon, sing the feem toon...

JEREMY: Well no, they've already got a song.

DENNIS: Yeah, I know it, (SINGS) 'They're bigger than most and tastier, de de de de de, that's why I'm the captain of the fish finger, de de de de de, they're called fish fingers (TRAILING OFF) but they're not fingers of fish because fish actually have fins.

JEREMY: Oh dear.

DENNIS: It's very hot today, isn't it?

WE SEE JEREMY PASSING A TINY HAND-HELD FAN ACROSS THE TABLE.

JEREMY: Well, why don't you try this.

TINY DENNIS HOLDS ON TO THE BOTTOM OF A GIANT FAN, AND BEGINS TO FLY AWAY.

DENNIS: Aaaaaaaah!

Oompa

UNIVERSITY OFFICE 3

INT: UNIVERSITY OFFICE. SITTING AT HER DESK, LINDA ANSWERS A KNOCK AT THE DOOR. PAUL, A YOUNG DWARF STUDENT, ENTERS.

LINDA: Come in, oh hello, Paul.

PAUL: Hello, I have the form right here, I just need the Head of Department to sign it.

LINDA MAKES A PHONE CALL.

LINDA: Ok, take a seat, I'll just see if he's in his office. Hello Martin, it's Linda, I've Paul Roberts here, needs you to sign his grant application form. You know Paul, everyone knows Paul. (PAUL LOOKS PLEASED) Um, shoulder length brown hair, wears a lot of jewellery . . . looks up a lot, gets his clothes from Mothercare. That's it, the Oompa Loompa. (TO PAUL) He says go straight up.

A STUNNED PAUL LEAVES THE ROOM.

LINDA: (SINGING TO HERSELF AS SHE WORKS) Oompa, Loompa, doobedy doo . . .

Loompa, doobedy doo . . .

MR MANN – VIDEO SHOP

INT: ROY IS STANDING BEHIND THE SHOP COUNTER. MR MANN ENTERS
THE SHOP.

TOM V/O: It's nought o'clock and at this shop in
Phlegm, Mr Mann is looking for a video. I
watched a video once, it was called Memorex
E180, it was rather dull.

ROY: Ah, actually I was just about to close for lu–.

MR MANN: (INTERRUPTS) It won't take long.

ROY: What is it you're looking for, ex–?

MR MANN: (INTERRUPTS) I would like to rent a film
staring Chevy Chase and Rick Moranis as a pair of
cops who have to go undercover and pose as rappers
in order to foil a drug deal, Certificate 15.

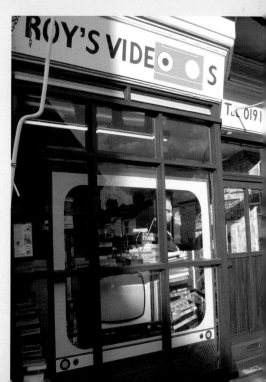

ROY: Oh, I don't think I know that film. But Margaret knows all the films, one moment. (SHOUTS) Margaret? Margaret?

LONG PAUSE. ROY AND MR MANN SHARE A POLITE SMILE.

MARGARET: (OFF-STAGE) Yes?

ROY: There's a gentleman here wants to know if we've got any videos starring Chevy Chase and Rick Moranis as a pair of cops who have to go undercover and pose as rappers in order to foil a drug deal.

MR MANN: Certificate 15.

ROY: (SHOUTS) Certificate 15.

MARGARET: Oh, I don't know.

ROY: (TURNING TO MR MANN) Oh, she doesn't know.

MR MANN: (UTTERLY DEADPAN) It actually ends up with them having to take part in a rap competition; it is very amusing.

MARGARET: (SHOUTS) Does he know what it's called?

ROY: Do you know what it's called?

MR MANN: No.

ROY: (SHOUTS) No.

MARGARET: Oh.

ROY: Oh. Well, I don't know what to suggest.

MARGARET: (SHOUTS) Is he sure the film exists?

ROY: Are you sure the film exists?

MR MANN: No.

ROY: (SHOUTS) No.

MR MANN: But it is the film I would like to see tonight.

ROY: Right. Well, I'm not sure it's been made, so I don't think you're going to be able to watch it tonight.

MR MANN: It's ok, I'll wait.

ROY: You, you'll wait?

Oh, I don't think I know that film.

But Margaret knows all the films,

one moment . . . .

Margaret?

Margaret?

MR MANN: Yes, until it's been made.

ROY: Well, here's an idea, how about we let you know the moment it comes in.

MR MANN: Yes, the moment please, I'm a very busy man.

THERE IS A LONG PAUSE. FINALLY, MR MANN'S MOBILE GOES OFF.

HE WAITS THREE LONG RINGS BEFORE ANSWERING IT.

MR MANN: Hello. Can I call you back? I'm just in the middle of something.

MR MANN HANGS UP AND CONTINUES TO WAIT.

MAGGIE AND JUDY — VOL-AU-VENTS

EXT: WOMEN'S INSTITUTE. WE SEE A SIGN, 'WOMEN'S INSTITUTE, POX VILLAGE BRANCH'.

TOM V/O: Today in Pox, the Women's Institute is playing host to their local conservative MP. I love the Conservatives; they're my favourite political party, after Labour and the Liberal Democrats.

INT: MAGGIE IS TALKING TO THE LOCAL MP AT A BUSY RECEPTION.

MAGGIE: Thank you so much for coming to talk to us today.

CONSERVATIVE MP: Oh, I wouldn't have missed it for the world, I know how important it is to have the support of you ladies.

JUDY JOINS MAGGIE AND THE MP WITH A PLATE OF VOL-AU-VENTS.

JUDY: Fancy a vol-au-vent?

CONSERVATIVE MP: Oh, yes please. Mm, that's delicious, did you make them yourself?

JUDY: Yes.

CONSERVATIVE MP: You must give me the recipe.

JUDY: Well, actually it's one of Ainsley Harriot's.

MAGGIE BEGINS TO HEAVE, BEFORE THROWING UP COPIOUSLY OVER THE MP.

MAGGIE: You really must come and speak to us again.

CONSERVATIVE MP: (COVERED IN VOMIT) Yes.

Fancy a vol-au-vent?

If you enjoy the smell of dung and being shouted at by farmers, why not spend a day in the countryside?

LOU AND ANDY — HORSE

EXT: A COUNTRY LANE. LOU IS PUSHING ANDY ALONG IN HIS WHEELCHAIR.

TOM V/O: If you enjoy the smell of dung and being shouted at by farmers, why not spend a day in the countryside?

LOU: Isn't the countryside lovely, Andrew?

ANDY: Boring.

LOU: But I thought you said you love the countryside. I thought you said that the natural world had a sublime beauty, unrivalled by anything manmade.

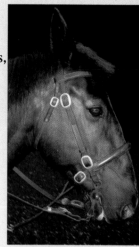

ANDY: Yeah, I know.

LOU: Now, where are we exactly?

LOU LOOKS AT HIS MAP.

ANDY: This is boring, I wanna go home.

A WOMAN ARRIVES ON HORSEBACK. LOU ASKS STOPS HER AND ASKS FOR DIRECTIONS.

LOU: Yeah, the trouble is, I think we're a bit lost. Let me just ask this lady. Er, excuse me love, I think we're a bit lost, um, do you know the way to, er, Taplow Farm?

HORSE RIDER: (DISMOUNTING) Ah, one moment.

LOU: Hello Mr Horse.

HORSE RIDER: Yeah, good boy.

LOU: He is a good boy isn't he, yes.

HORSE RIDER: Right let's have a look now, Taplow Farm, it's quite a way.

LOU: Yeah it's here on the map, I thought we were near it.

WHILE THEY CONTINUE TO TALK AND LOOK AT THE MAP, ANDY GETS OUT OF HIS WHEELCHAIR, JUMPS ON THE HORSE AND RIDES OFF ACROSS THE FIELD.

HORSE RIDER: Now we're the yellow line marked here.

LOU: Oh, I thought we were coming along this way.

HORSE RIDER: No, no.

WE SEE ANDY DISAPPEARING INTO THE DISTANCE ON HORSEBACK. LOU AND THE HORSE RIDER REMAIN BLISSFULLY UNAWARE.

TOM V/O: And so we conclude our journey around Little Britain. Tonight's program has ended a little sooner than usual, because I need to do a poo now. Good bye bye.

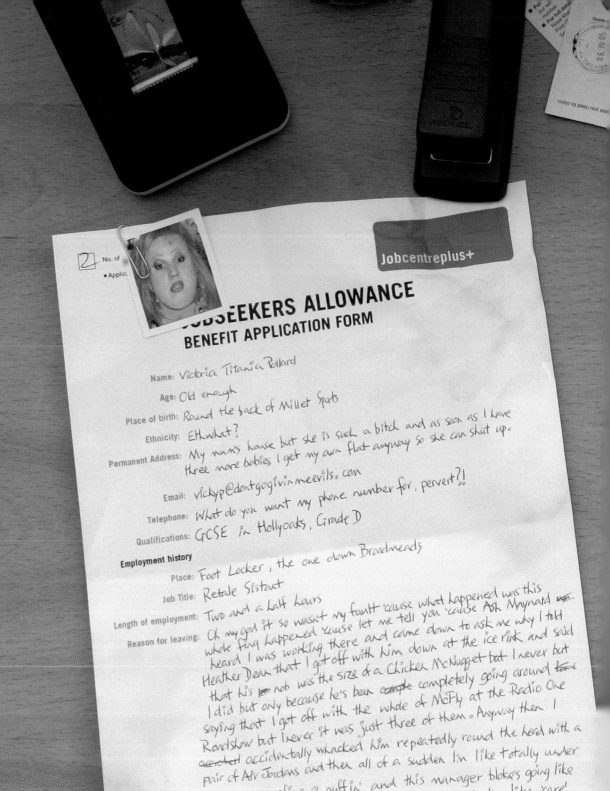

No. of

• Applic

JOBSEEKERS ALLOWANCE

BENEFIT APPLICATION FORM

Name: Victoria Titania Pollard

Age: Old enough

Place of birth: Round the back of Millet Sports

Ethnicity: Eh what?

Permanent Address: My mum's house but she is such a bitch and as soon as I have three more babies I get my own flat anyway so she can shut up.

Email: vickyp@dontgogivinmeevils.com

Telephone: What do you want my phone number for, pervert?!

Qualifications: GCSE in Hollyoaks, Grade D

Employment history

Place: Foot Locker, the one down Broadmeads

Job Title: Retale Sistant

Length of employment: Two and a half hours

Reason for leaving: Oh my god it so wasn't my fault 'cause what happened was this whole fing happened 'cause let me tell you 'cause Ash Maynard heard I was working there and came down to ask me why I told Heather Dean that I got off with him down at the ice rink and said that his nob was the size of a Chicken McNugget but I never but I did but only because he's been completely going around saying that I got off with the whole of McFly at the Radio One Roadshow but I never it was just three of them. Anyway then I accidentally whacked him repeatedly round the head with a pair of Air Jordans and then all of a sudden I'm like totally under arrest or somefing or nuffin' and this manager bloke's going like he don't want me working there anymore and I'm like 'care' 'cause I'm actually down to the last twenty in the Cotham heats of Channel Five's 'Make Me A Supermodel' anyway 'cause I'm like well fit so get over it, you winging spacker.

Office use only: do not write below this line

Corr. no: **Ref:**

code: **Area:**

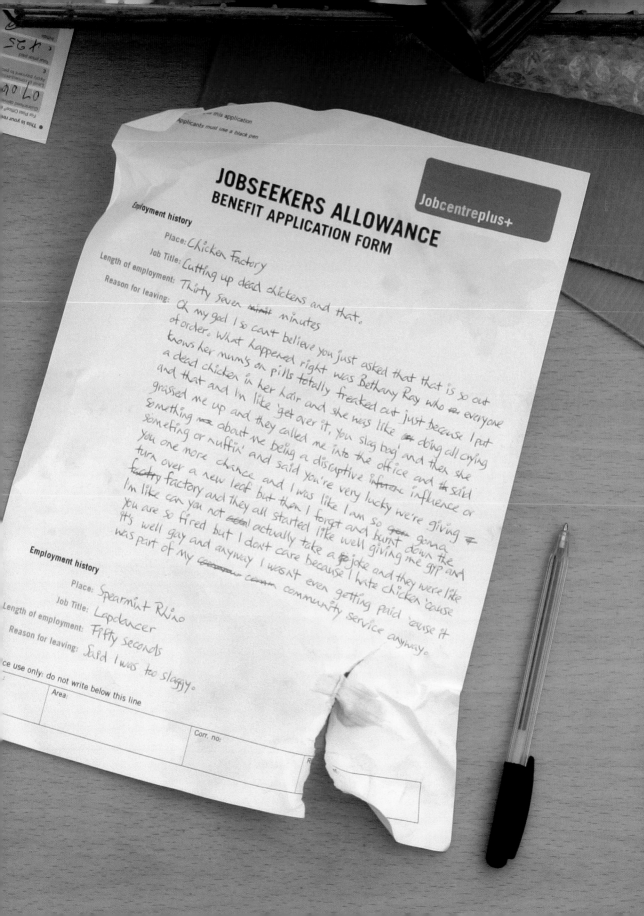

JOBSEEKERS ALLOWANCE
BENEFIT APPLICATION FORM

Jobcentreplus+

Employment history

Place: Chicken Factory

Job Title: Cutting up dead chickens and that.

Length of employment: Thirty seven ~~minut~~ minutes

Reason for leaving: Oh my god I so can't believe you just asked that that is so out of order. What happened right was Bethany Ray who ~~ev~~ everyone knows her mum's on pills totally freaked out just because I put a dead chicken in her hair and she was like 'get over it, you slag bag' and then she grassed me up and they called me into the office and ~~the~~ said and that and I'm like ~~did~~ doing all crying something ~~no~~ about me being a disruptive ~~influ~~ influence or something or nuffin' and said you're very lucky we're giving you one more chance and I was like I am so ~~gon~~ gonna turn over a new leaf but then I forgot and burnt down the ~~factor~~ factory and they all started like well giving me gyp and I'm like can you not ~~eel~~ actually take a ~~pe~~joke and they were like you are so fired but I don't care because I hate chicken 'cause it's well gay and anyway I wasn't even getting paid 'cause it was part of my ~~commun~~ community service anyway.

Employment history

Place: Spearmint Rhino

Job Title: Lapdancer

Length of employment: Fifty seconds

Reason for leaving: Said I was too slaggy.

~~Offi~~ce use only: do not write below this line

Area:

Corr. no:

EPISODE

TOM V/O: Britain, Britain, Britain, cultural capital of the world. The Sistine Chapel, British. Mozart's Requiem, British. The Great Wall of China, British. But none of that stuff would have even been invented were it not for the people of Britain, the men, the women, the boys, the girls and the monkey children that populate this well fit country. Let's 'ave it!

VICKY POLLARD — BUS

EXT: BUS. VICKY AND HER FRIEND ARE SMOKING ON THE TOP FLOOR OF A DOUBLE-DECKER BUS.

TOM V/O: Vicky Pollard hates smoking, except in places where it is prohibited.

BUS CONDUCTOR: Put that cigarette out, please.

VICKY SULLENLY LOWERS HER HAND AND APPEARS TO PUT HER CIGARETTE OUT. ALMOST IMMEDIATELY, SHE LIFTS HER OTHER HAND TO HER MOUTH AND TAKES A DRAG FROM A SECOND CIGARETTE.

BUS CONDUCTOR: And that one. See your ticket, please.

VICKY: Yeah I got my ticket . . . right here!

VICKY REACHES INTO HER JACKET POCKET AS IF TO TAKE OUT A TICKET, AND INSTEAD SHOWS THE CONDUCTOR HER MIDDLE FINGER.

BUS CONDUCTOR: Alright, I've warned you before, if you don't have a ticket you're gonna have to get off.

VICKY: Oh my God that is so unfair this is like well sexual harassment. If you like fancy me why don't you just say so. God this is exactly like the time Miss Rennet who everyone knows is a total lesbian made Candice Burton stay behind after PE and started telling her off for gobbing on Samina Geshwani's hair but everyone knows she only made her stay late because she wanted to get off with her 'cause when she was telling her off her legs were wide open and Candice reckons she could see her spider.

BUS CONDUCTOR: Right, you don't have a ticket, you can get off at the next stop.

VICKY'S FRIEND: It's OK Vicky, I got you a ticket, one for you, one for me.

BUS CONDUCTOR: Thank you.

VICKY: What you do that for you total virgin?! I don't need no ticket to get on no bus I'm

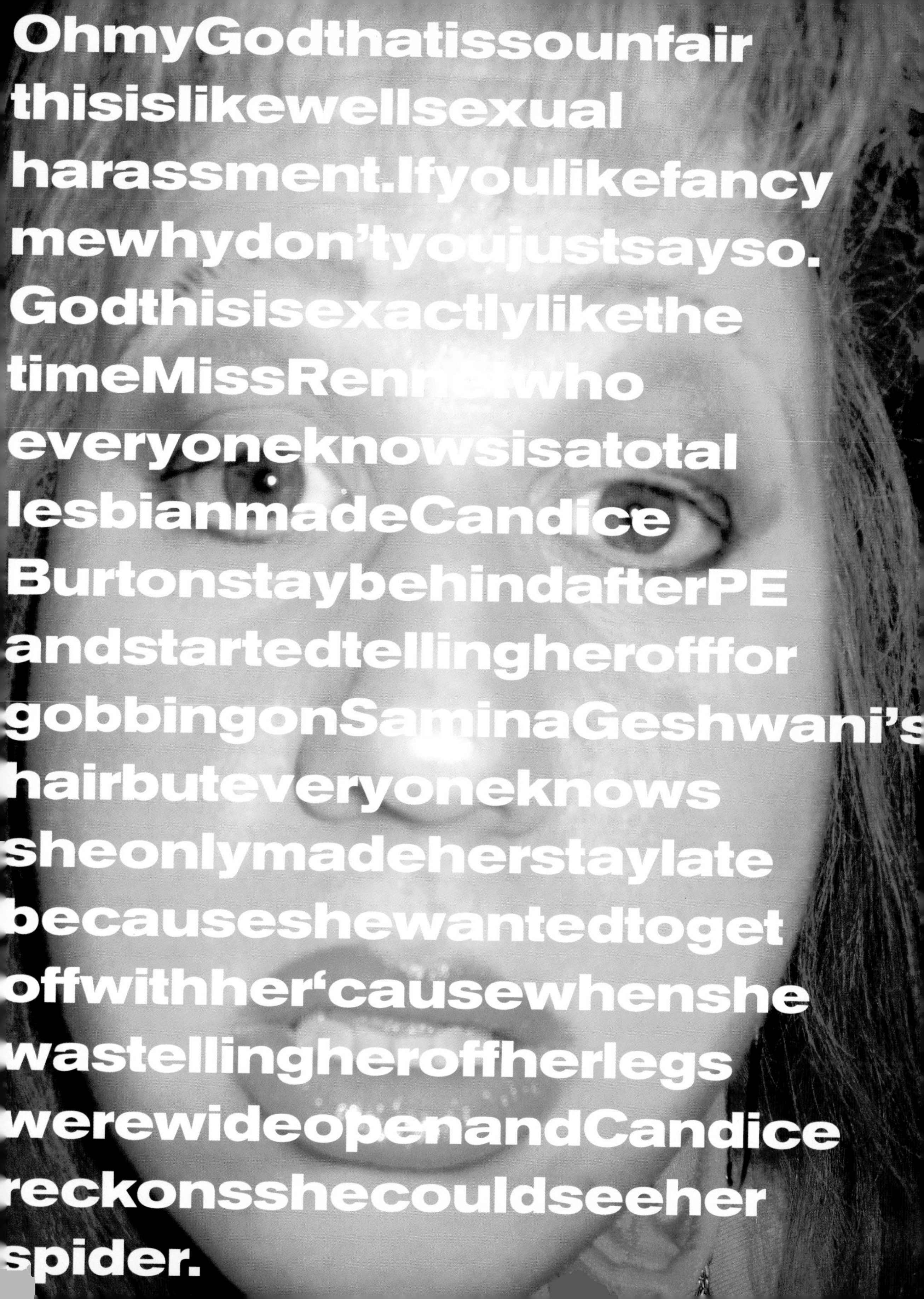

OhmyGodthatissounfair
thisislikewellsexual
harassment.Ifyoulikefancy
mewhydon'tyoujustsayso.
Godthisisexactlylikethe
timeMissRennetwho
everyoneknowsisatotal
lesbianmadeCandice
BurtonstaybehindafterPE
andstartedtellingherofffor
gobbingonSaminaGeshwani's
hairbuteveryoneknows
sheonlymadeherstaylate
becauseshewantedtoget
offwithher'causewhenshe
wastellingheroffherlegs
werewideopenandCandice
reckonsshecouldseeher
spider.

Vicky Pollard. Oh my God if anyone hears about this they're gonna think I'm well sad. This is like the time Tony Tozer told the whole of the Fourth Year that I shat myself on a field trip to the ancient city of Bath it wasn't me it was Bernice Donnelly and I can prove it because I made a tape of her crying and admitting it and anyone says I'm not hard is well gonna get spannered.

VICKY'S FRIEND: Sorry Vicky, it don't look like we're gonna get chucked off now.

VICKY: That's what you reckon.

VICKY TAKES OUT A MARKER PEN AND BEGINS TO WRITE ON THE WINDOW... 'F . . U . . . C . . '

BUS CONDUCTOR: Oi!

VICKY: Haven't finished yet. So rude.

LOU AND ANDY — ICE SKATING

EXT: ICE-SKATING RINK. LOU IS PUTTING ON A PAIR OF ICE SKATES WHILE ANDY WATCHES THE SKATERS FROM HIS WHEELCHAIR.

TOM V/O: Meanwheel, in Herby . . .

LOU: Now, you sure you don't mind just sitting here for a bit and watching?

ANDY: Yeah.

LOU: You sure?

ANDY: Yeah.

LOU: 'Cause last time we came here you said it was boring. You said that Torville and Dean's Barnum routine aside, ice skating was aesthetically bankrupt.

ANDY: Yeah, I know.

LOU TAKES OUT TWO ENORMOUS BAGS OF CRISPS, AND HOLDS THEM UP.

LOU: Alright, I'll only be twenty minutes or so. Oh, erm . . . which crisps do you want?

ANDY: (POINTING WITHOUT LOOKING) I want that one.

LOU: The cheese and the onion, right.

ANDY: (POINTING AT THE OTHER BAG, STILL NOT LOOKING) And I want that one.

LOU GIVES HIM BOTH BAGS, GETS UP AND MAKES HIS WAY ONTO THE ICE.

LOU: Right. See you in a bit, then. Oh, wish me luck.

OUT ON THE ICE LOU FLAILS AROUND, TRYING HIS BEST TO STAY UPRIGHT BEFORE FINALLY GRABBING HOLD OF THE BARRIER TO REST.

LOU: Ah, just catch me breath. Oh, what a kerfuffle. Come on Lou, you can do this . . .

IN THE BACKGROUND, WE SEE ANDY SAIL NONCHALANTLY BY ON SKATES, EATING FROM A BIG BAG OF CRISPS AS HE GOES.

EPISODE three

'Cause last time we came here you said it was boring. You said that Torville and Dean's Barnum routine aside, ice skating was aesthetically bankrupt.

Ooh, he was **GORGEOUS**. Lovely, he was. He had lovely long hair and he was wearing these tight jeans and at one point he looked at me, I thought I was gonna melt, ooh he was a nosh.

VIV – JEWELLERY SHOP ROBBERY

EXT: JEWELLER'S. THERE HAS OBVIOUSLY BEEN A BREAK-IN. WE SEE A FORENSICS OFFICER SLIPPING UNDER THE POLICE BARRIERS AND INTO THE SHOP, WHILE TWO POLICE OFFICERS, WITH THEIR BACKS TO US, ARE BUSY INVESTIGATING THE BROKEN WINDOW. THEY TURN ROUND LOOKING VERY PLEASED WITH THEMSELVES, WEARING WOMEN'S EARRINGS, BRACELETS AND NECKLACES FROM THE SMASHED WINDOW.

TOM V/O: At this jeweller's in Gristle, a robbery has just taken place.

INT: JEWELLER'S SHOP. WHILE THE FORENSICS OFFICER TAKES FINGERPRINTS, THE CAMERA PANS ROUND TO REVEAL A POLICE INSPECTOR QUESTIONING VIV.

POLICE INSPECTOR: So Viv, you were standing here at the time of the robbery when three men came in. Now one of them we know was carrying a gun, can you say what he looked like?

VIV: Ooh, he was *gorgeous*. Lovely, he was. He had lovely long hair and he was wearing these tight jeans and at one point he looked at me, I thought I was gonna melt, ooh he was a *nosh*.

POLICE INSPECTOR: And did you get a good look at the second man?

VIV: Yes I did, ooh, he was *gorgeous*, he was a bit short and he wasn't what I normally go for 'cause I like 'em tall, just like you, but ooh, he was *gorgeous* and he had this voice that was like (GRUFFLY) 'put the money in the bag and no one will get hurt', ooh, he reminds me of a young Patrick Mower, mmm.

POLICE INSPECTOR: And the third man?

VIV: Ooh, he was *gorgeous*, black he was but that don't bother me, phwoar, ooh he was, what's the word?

POLICE INSPECTOR: Gorgeous?

VIV: Hands off, I've seen him first, ooh he was lush, I would have very much liked to have sex with him.

POLICE INSPECTOR: Alright, thank you, one last question: did you get a look at the getaway driver?

VIV: Oh, was there a getaway driver?

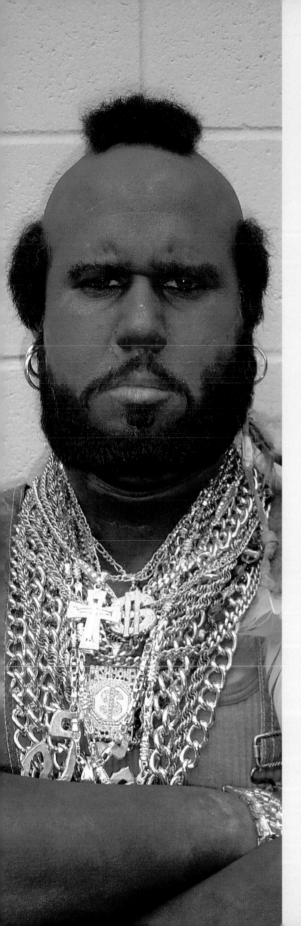

POLICE INSPECTOR: Yes there was, he was parked outside the shop in a (CHECKS HIS NOTES) metallic blue Vauxhall Corsa.

VIV: Ooh, I'm not sure whether I . . . now come on, Viv, think, this is important . . . I must have done, because I saw them run out and you're right, they got into a blue car and there was a man sitting in the front seat and . . . ooh he was *gorgeous*.

MR T

EXT: LEISURE CENTRE. THE CAMERA PANS ROUND THE GYM TO SHOW PEOPLE EXERCISING ON VARIOUS MACHINES.

TOM V/O: To keep fit, people in Britain go to gymnasia. I don't need to take exercise as I have the body of an Adonis.

WE SEE A MAN WHO IS THE SPITTING IMAGE OF MR T, WITH A MOHICAN AND LOTS OF GOLD CHAINS, SITTING ON A PIECE OF EQUIPMENT, LIFTING WEIGHTS. ANOTHER MAN IS KEEN TO USE THE SAME MACHINE, AND STRIKES UP A CONVERSATION.

MAN: Alright?

MR T: (IN A NORMAL, UNASSUMING BRITISH VOICE) Yeah.

MAN: Are you using this?

MR T: Yeah, I've just got one more set to do.

MAN: (TENTATIVELY) You must get this all the time, but I tell you who you look like: Mr T.

MR T: Who?

MAN: Mr T, you know, the bloke out of *The A Team*.

MR T: Oh, I haven't seen it.

MAN: You must know him, though, he's the guy with the mohican and the gold chains, he was in *Rocky* as well.

MR T: Oh, not Sylvester Stallone?

You must get this all the time, but I tell you who you look like: **Mr T**.

MAN: No, his name's Mr T. Honestly, he looks just like you.

MR T: (UNINTERESTED) Oh, well I'll look out for him.

MAN: (POINTING) Is that yours?

MR T: Oh . . . Cheers.

MR T BENDS TO HIS RIGHT AND PICKS UP A GLASS OF MILK THAT HAD BEEN SITTING ON THE FLOOR BY HIS MACHINE.

EXT: LEISURE CENTRE. THE SECOND MAN IS WALKING DOWN THE PATH TO THE CAR PARK, FOLLOWED BY MR T.

MR T: Oh, what's that show called again?

MAN: *The A Team.*

MR T: *The A Team*, right.

THE MAN AND MR T WALK TOWARDS THEIR RESPECTIVE CARS.

Oh yeah, and it's Mr P, yeah?

MAN: Yeah, I think they sometimes show it on UK Gold.

MR T: Oh yeah, and it's Mr P, yeah?

MAN: No, it's Mr T.

MR T GETS INTO HIS A TEAM BLACK VAN AND CLOSES THE DOOR.

MR T: Mr T, right. See ya.

EMILY AND FLORENCE – FOOTBALL

EXT: EMILY AND FLORENCE ARE OUT WALKING IN THE FIELDS TOGETHER WITH THEIR PARASOLS.

TOM V/O: Men dressing up in women's clothing is, in my view, a disgusting perversion. Yes I'm sitting here in bra and panties, but I draw the line there.

FLORENCE: Two ladies!

EMILY: My lady, my lady, out for a stroll.

FLORENCE: Not men, definitely not men.

WE SEE A GROUP OF YOUNG BOYS HAVING A KICKAROUND ON THE PLAYING FIELDS.

EMILY: Oh Florence, regardez les enfants playing . . . footie.

FLORENCE: Oh, how enchanting. Of course you used to play football, didn't you?

EMILY: (GIRLISHLY, EMBARRASSED) Oh, no no.

FLORENCE: You did, you were Left Back for QPR.

EMILY: Florence, please remember, I'm a lady.

TWO YOUNG BOYS WALK OVER.

BOY: Here mate, can we have our ball back, please?

FLORENCE: Leave it, Emily.

FLORENCE AND EMILY WALK TOWARDS THE FOOTBALL; EMILY IS CLEARLY TRYING HARD TO RESIST THE TEMPTATION
TO KICK THE BALL.

EMILY: Florence, I can't help it.

FLORENCE: Fight it, Emily!

EMILY: I can't, ooh!

EMILY PROCEEDS TO TAKE THE BALL AND DRIBBLE ROUND ALL OF THE BOYS ON THE FOOTBALL PITCH.

FLORENCE: Be strong Emily, think of ladies' things. Oh!

EMILY SCORES AND WHEELS AWAY IN TRIUMPH, CHEERING LIKE A BLOKE. THE BOYS WATCH DUMBFOUNDED AS
EMILY AND FLORENCE RECOVER THEIR COMPOSURE AND WALK AWAY.

EMILY: I think we got away with that. *Au revoir.*

THEY QUICKEN THEIR STEP AND BREAK INTO A RUN.

MARJORIE DAWES/FATFIGHTERS — LOTTERY

INT: FATFIGHTERS MEETING. MARJORIE IS ADDRESSING THE MEMBERS.

TOM V/O: If I had my way, fat people would be strangled at birth, but unfortunately they're permitted to live.

MARJORIE: Anyway, before we start proper some congratulations are in order, aren't they Meera, because, FatFighters, we have a National Lottery winner in our midst. Not the

jackpot, that went to a white man, but Meera Sharma, I am pronouncing it right aren't I, chose correctly five numbers plus the bonus ball and won herself two hundred and fourteen thousand pounds! (THE FATFIGHTERS APPLAUD) How about that. Anyway, what I think is

. . . we have a National Lottery winner in our midst. Not the jackpot, that went to a white man, but Meera Sharma, I am pronouncing it right aren't I . . . Anyway, what I think is important is that none of us here treats her any differently, isn't that right my beautiful Asian friend?

important is that none of us here treats her any differently, isn't that right my beautiful Asian friend?

MEERA: Yes, Marjorie

MARJORIE: Yes, Marjorie, perfect English, well done, because a lot of them don't make the effort. Now, before we go any further: last week I gave you all the new, they are new, FatFighters diet sheets to fill out or fill in, so can I have them back, please. Thank you, Paul. Ryvita for breakfast, yeah right, what did you have on it, lard?

MARJORIE: No one likes a liar Paul. (TAKING TANIA'S SHEET) Thank you. It says here you had fruit for lunch . . .

TANIA: That's right.

MARJORIE: What was it, chocolate orange? Eh, chocolate orange? I don't know, you fatties.

MARJORIE WALKS ALONG THE LINE TO MEERA, HOLDING OUT ONE OF THE SHEETS FOR A LADY IN THE FRONT ROW TO SMELL.

MARJORIE: Ooh that smells lovely, have a sniff of that. Yes, 'cause a lot of people say they smell funny but I don't think so, no, I'm all for Asians. Ooh where'd you get your safari

Marjorie's weekly Diet Sheet.

Date Fifteen of November
Name ~~Merra~~ / ~~Mici~~ / ~~Miller~~
ASIAN WOMAN

	Break fast	lunch	Dinner	TREat
Monday	Bowl of dust, with a splash of dust.	Dust sandwich.	Grilled breast of dust, with a dust salad. No dressing.	particle of dust.
tuesday	Two slices of toasted dust, lightly spread with dust .	Dust soup.	Dust pie, followed by Dust sorbet.	Dust tortilla with dust dip.
Wednesday	Half a fresh dust-fruit.	FatFighters Dust Shake (available in Chocolate, Vanilla or Dust flavours).	Poached dust in a white wine sauce.	Raw dust.
Thur sday	Hard-boiled dust.	Dust casserole with dust dumplings.	Deep-fried dust in breadcrumbs. To drink: can of Diet Dust.	Short suck on a duster.
Friday	Full English dust.	Dustburger.	Dust goujons.	Slice of low-cal dustcake (see my noo recipe sheet: 101 Things To Do With Dust) and a cup of dust tea, but with no extra dust.
Saturday	Pain au dust.	Fillet of dust, oven-cooked with a dust crust.	Boil- in-the-bag dust with a medley of dust.	Lick of the skirting board.
Sunday	Smoked dust.	Roast dust with all the trimmings .	Stir-fried dust.	Chew on a dust sheet.

It's not easy but good luck and remember — you are fat, loathsome scum.

Happy dieting, Fat Fighters.

Marjorie

from? I'd love one of them, and one of them red dots, they're brilliant. And ain't you got lovely handwriting? Just as well, you'll be writing a lot of cheques now no doubt, for all your family in India.

MEERA: New Malden.

MARJORIE: And have you thought what you're gonna do with it yet? I tell you what I'd do, I'd pay off me mortgage, yeah, I'd go on holiday and the rest of it I'd share with my friends here at FatFighters, is that what you're gonna do, or . . .

MEERA: I haven't decided.

MARJORIE: She hasn't decided yet so just slow down you lot, honestly.

MEERA: Please, stop mentioning it.

MARJORIE: Yeah, please can we all please now stop mentioning it? Dear oh dear Meera, they're like a pack of vultures. Sorry Meera, vulture, it's a type of bird, like chicken balti but without the balti. Right, come on, 'cause we've gotta get through this now. (RETURNING TO THE SUBJECT OF DIET SHEETS) So, One: Breakfast . . . actually I will just say, sorry, it's playing

> # Now, these . . . I spend — I do my numbers on a Saturday, I do five lucky dip mid-week, I do scratchcards and I haven't won a penny and I have lived in this country all my life. Basically Meera it's THEFT, what you have done is THEFT. Horrible how a lottery win changes someone, innit?

on me mind, Mum's not well again and all she wants really is one last trip to Barbados but, money ain't it, mmm, eh? Ain't that right my gorgeous Asian lady? Money money money, give it to me . . .

AN AWKWARD SILENCE FROM THE FATFIGHTERS.

MARJORIE: (UNABLE TO CONTROL HER FRUSTRATION) Now, these diet sheets . . . I spend – I do my numbers on a Saturday, I do five lucky dip mid-week, I do scratchcards and I haven't won a penny and I have lived in this country all my life. Basically Meera it's theft, what you have done is theft. Horrible how a lottery win changes someone, innit?

SEBASTIAN AND MICHAEL — ANDREW

EXT: 10 DOWNING STREET. SEBASTIAN IS STANDING IN THE DOORWAY OF NO. 10, THROWING PAPERS AND A BRIEFCASE OUT ON TO THE STREET. A FLUSTERED CHANCELLOR OF THE EXCHEQUER IS FORCED TO SCRABBLE AROUND ON THE PAVEMENT TO COLLECT HIS THINGS.

TOM V/O: No.10 is a hive of activity. Following a hostile meeting with the Chancellor of the Exchequer, the Prime Minister and his aide Sebastian are hard at it.

THE PRIME MINISTER IS FACING US, STANDING. SEBASTIAN IS KNEELING DOWN IN FRONT OF HIM, AT CROTCH LEVEL. WE SEE THE BACK OF SEBASTIAN'S HEAD BOBBING AWAY BUSILY, HIS HANDS HIDDEN FROM VIEW BUT CLEARLY FIDDLING WITH SOMETHING.

MICHAEL: Are you going to be long, Sebastian?

SEBASTIAN: Sorry, Prime Minister, my mouth's a bit full . . . Finished.

THE CAMERA PANS ROUND TO REVEAL SEBASTIAN WITH A NEEDLE AND THREAD.

MICHAEL: I didn't even realize there was a tear.

SEBASTIAN REACHES OUT A FINGER AND, TOO SLOWLY AND FOR TOO LONG, LIGHTLY STROKES THE FRONT OF MICHAEL'S TROUSERS.

SEBASTIAN: Yeah, it's right there, Prime Minister.

AFTER AN AWKWARD PAUSE, SEBASTIAN STANDS UP AND FOLLOWS THE PRIME MINISTER TO HIS DESK. HE STANDS FAR TOO CLOSELY TO THE PRIME MINISTER'S BACK, AS HE CHECKS HIS NOTES.

SEBASTIAN: Oh, erm, here are the notes from the Russian trade negotiations, Prime Minister.

MICHAEL: Erm, who am I meeting?

SEBASTIAN IS STARING INTENTLY AT THE BACK OF THE PRIME MINISTER'S HEAD, ROCKING HIS BODY EVER SO SLIGHTLY, LOST IN HIS THOUGHTS.

SEBASTIAN: Oh, erm, some envoy from the British Embassy in Moscow.

MICHAEL: You'd better show him in.

SEBASTIAN MAKES A NOISE, 'POP!', AS HE COMES TO FROM HIS FANTASY AND TURNS TO WALK TO THE DOOR.

SEBASTIAN: OK . . . (OPENING THE DOOR) The Prime Minister will see you now.

EPISODE *three*

Sorry, Prime Minister, my mouth's a bit full . . .

A GOOD-LOOKING YOUNG MAN IN A WELL-CUT SUIT ENTERS THE ROOM.

ANDREW: (AFFECTIONATELY) Michael.

MICHAEL: (CLEARLY DELIGHTED AT THE SURPRISE) Andrew, I had no idea it was you, how the devil are you?

ANDREW AND MICHAEL SHAKE HANDS HEARTILY. CLEARLY JEALOUS, SEBASTIAN HITS THEIR HANDS APART, PETULANTLY.

SEBASTIAN: Can you not touch him, please!

MICHAEL: Oh Sebastian, it's quite alright, this is Andrew Wiltshire, actually he had your job, oh, how many years ago?

ANDREW: Well, nearly five years ago.

MICHAEL: Five years, oh God, it's good to see you!

ANDREW AND THE PRIME MINISTER EMBRACE, OR TRY TO, SINCE SEBASTIAN FURIOUSLY TRIES TO PULL THEM APART.

SEBASTIAN: (LAUGHING MANICALLY) Ha ha ha ha ha!

MICHAEL: So now you're in Moscow?

ANDREW: Yes, yes.

MICHAEL: Well how have you been?

ANDREW: Well fine, obviously not quite as much fun as working for you . . . no staying up the night of the by-election drinking tequila.

MICHAEL: (CHUCKLING AT THE MEMORY) Don't remind me.

SEBASTIAN: (JEALOUSLY) What was that?

MICHAEL: We just spent some very funny drunken evenings together.

SEBASTIAN: What happened?

MICHAEL: Nothing happened, we just got very drunk and . . .

ANDREW: Oh, what about that time you locked yourself out of your room and knocked at my door at three o'clock in the morning.

ANDREW AND MICHAEL BOTH LAUGH FONDLY AT THE RECOLLECTION.

SEBASTIAN: Were you naked?

ANDREW: No . . .

Were you naked?

Prime Minister, I'd really appreciate it if you didn't invite your exes round. It makes me feel very uncomfortable.

SEBASTIAN: What happened then?

MICHAEL: Oh, it's a long story.

SEBASTIAN: Let's hear it.

ANDREW: Yes, well, maybe we should get down to business, Prime Minister.

SEBASTIAN: Yeah, the Prime Minister's actually very busy, so if you could sort of get to the point.

ANDREW BEGINS TO FOLLOW THE PRIME MINISTER TO HIS DESK, WHILE SEBASTIAN ATTEMPTS TO BAR HIS PROGRESS.

ANDREW: Right, yes, well, er, maybe the best thing is if you can take a look at these documents . . . and sign them off before I leave on Friday.

MICHAEL: You're here till Friday?

ANDREW: Yes. Well, I've got some free time if you fancy a drink in the Commons bar, a bit of a catch up.

SEBASTIAN: No, we're very busy.

SEBASTIAN TAKES A FIRM HOLD OF THE PRIME MINISTER'S SHOULDERS, PROPRIETORIALLY.

MICHAEL: (WINCING) You're hurting, Sebastian.

ANDREW: Right, well, I'll see you at the end of the week.

THE PRIME MINISTER STANDS UP TO SHAKE ANDREW'S HAND.

MICHAEL: Great to see you.

SEBASTIAN BREAKS THE HANDSHAKE AND STARTS TO CAJOLE ANDREW OUT OF THE OFFICE.

ANDREW: Great to see you, too. And nice to meet you, Sebastian.

SEBASTIAN PUSHES ANDREW OUT OF THE DOOR.

SEBASTIAN: Yeah, whatever! (SEBASTIAN SHUTS THE DOOR) Prime Minister, I'd really appreciate it if you didn't invite your exes round. It makes me feel very uncomfortable.

EPISODE *three*

MICHAEL: (STERNLY) Sebastian, I really need to read these papers.

CRESTFALLEN, SEBASTIAN TURNS AWAY, BUT IS CLEARLY ITCHING TO SAY SOMETHING. FINALLY, HE TURNS BACK ROUND.

SEBASTIAN: Did you sleep with him?

KENNY CRAIG – THUNDERCATS

EXT: HOUSE ON AN ORDINARY, LEAFY STREET. THE CAMERA PANS ACROSS TO SHOW A POSTER OF A DOG, ATTACHED TO A TREE: 'HAVE YOU SEEN THIS CAT? PLEASE CALL 01632 850314.'

TOM V/O: This is the house that stage hypnotist Kenny Craig shares with his mother. I still live with my mother, although she died many years ago.

INT: LIVING ROOM. KENNY IS SITTING ON THE SOFA, UTTERLY ABSORBED IN A TELEVISION PROGRAMME. HIS ELDERLY MOTHER COMES INTO THE ROOM CARRYING A CUP OF TEA.

KENNY'S MOTHER: There you go, love. (SITTING DOWN, OBVIOUSLY GRATEFUL FOR THE REST) Oh . . . oh I forgot the sugar, you couldn't be a love and get it, could you?

KENNY: (FRUSTRATED, NOT LOOKING AWAY FROM THE TELEVISION) Mum, *Thundercats*!

KENNY'S MOTHER: But I just sat down.

KENNY: (HYPNOTIZING HER)) Look into my eyes, look into my eyes, the eyes, the eyes, not round the eyes, don't look around the eyes, look into my eyes (CLICKS HIS FINGERS), you're under. You may be old and recovering from double hip surgery but you're still perfectly

capable of getting up and bringing in the sugar bowl, honestly – three – two – one – you're back in the room.

KENNY'S MOTHER: (BRIGHTLY) Oh, I'll just go and get the sugar.

KENNY: (CALLING AFTER HER) And I know you've got some orange viscounts in there so can you bring those in, please.(MUTTERING TO HIMSELF) Very lazy person . . .

KENNY'S MOTHER RETURNS WITH THE SUGAR AND BISCUITS, THEN LOOKS AT HER WATCH.

KENNY'S MOTHER: Here you are. Oh, what time is it? *Songs of Praise* is on the other side.

KENNY: (TURNING AWAY FROM THE TV, ANNOYED) Look into my eyes. Look into my eyes. The eyes. The eyes. Not around the eyes. Don't look around the eyes. Look into my eyes, you're

under. This is, like, an all-time classic episode of *Thundercats*, I'm quite frankly
astounded that you'd rather watch *Songs of Praise*, which is just all about God, three –
two – one – in fact you now don't believe in God any more, so you won't want to watch
it ever again, three – two – one – you're back in the room.

KENNY'S MOTHER: Ah, just stick with *Thunderbirds*, shall we?

KENNY: Thunder*cats*.

KENNY'S MOTHER: Thunder what?

KENNY: (EXASPERATED) Urgh, look into my eyes. Look into my eyes. *Thundercats*, Urgh!

KENNY'S MOTHER: *Thundercats*?

KENNY: Yes, good.

KENNY'S MOTHER: Well, you're going to have to turn it off soon, 'cause I've got the girls
coming round later for gin rummy.

KENNY: Oh, give me strength. Look into my eyes. Look into my eyes. All around my eyes . . .

KENNY'S MOTHER: Sorry, love, can I just get me glasses, it might work better with them
on. Right, ready!

DR LAWRENCE AND ANNE – FEEDING THE DUCKS

EXT: AERIAL SHOT OF A PARK. THE CAMERA PANS DOWN TO SHOW THE TWO DOCTORS AND ANNE WALKING BESIDE THE RIVER.

TOM V/O: It's five to Gill and Dr Lawrence is showing Dr Beagrie some of the work he does outside of the hospital.

DR LAWRENCE: Usually Anne likes to come down to this park, and I encourage it. Just a simple thing like feeding the ducks can be very calming.

ANNE STANDS BY THE LAKE, HOLDING A PLASTIC BAG, SQUAWKING WHILE THROWING WHOLE LOAVES OF BREAD AGGRESSIVELY INTO THE WATER.

ANNE: Eh eh eh!

DR LAWRENCE: Anne loves those ducks.

ANNE: (STILL THROWING LOAVES) Eh eh eh!

DR LAWRENCE: She's always feeding them.

SHE HURLS A PACKET OF BISCUITS.

ANNE: Eh eh eh!

DR LAWRENCE: I don't know if Anne has a favourite duck, you'd have to ask her.

SHE EMPTIES THE BAG.

ANNE: Eh eh eh!

DR LAWRENCE: There used to be some swans round here, you don't see them any more.

EPISODE *three*

ANNE STOPS THROWING BREAD, LIFTS UP HER SKIRT AND
BEGINS TO URINATE INTO THE WATER, ALL THE WHILE
WALKING UP AND DOWN THE BANK OF THE LAKE.

DR LAWRENCE: (THOUGHTFULLY) I suppose Anne
is just one of those people who loves wildlife.

MR MANN –
NEWSAGENT'S

INT: NEWSAGENT'S.

TOM V/O: It's nought o'clock, and at this
shop in Phlegm, Mr Mann is looking for a
birthday card. I had a birthday once. I was
forty-four.

I don't have any arms or legs.

 # Sorry, Margaret, I forgot.

ROY IS STANDING IN HIS USUAL POSITION, BEHIND THE COUNTER. MR MANN ENTERS THE SHOP AND LIMPS SLOWLY
AND DELIBERATELY UP TO THE COUNTER.

MR MANN: Hello.

ROY: Hello. Erm, sorry, I was just about to take my lunch hour. Erm, (SHOUTS) Margaret?
Margaret? . . .

THERE FOLLOWS A VERY LONG, UNCOMFORTABLE PAUSE. THE PAIR EXCHANGE POLITE SMILES.

MARGARET: (OFF STAGE) Yes?

ROY: I was just about to take my lunch hour, can you come downstairs and serve the
gentleman?

MARGARET: I don't have any arms or legs.

ROY: (SHOUTS) Sorry, Margaret, I forgot.

ROY: (TO MR MANN) So, er, how can I help –.

MR MANN: (INTERRUPTS) Oh yes, I would like to purchase a birthday card, please.

ROY: (INDICATING A VARIETY OF CARDS ON THE COUNTER) Right, well, these are all birthday cards–

MR MANN: For a man.

ROY: Right, well, these are the men's cards–

MR MANN: Who is sixty . . .

ROY BEGINS TO HOLD UP A 60TH-BIRTHDAY CARD.

MR MANN: . . . five.

ROY HOLDS UP A CARD WITH 'HAPPY 65TH BIRTHDAY' AND A DOG ON THE FRONT.

MR MANN: He hates dogs . . .

ROY STARTS TO HOLD UP A CARD WITH A CAT ON INSTEAD.

MR MANN: And cats . . .

ROY HOLDS UP A CARD WITH A FROG ON IT.

MR MANN: And cartoon frogs . . .

ROY: Does he hate all animals?

MR MANN: No, he likes single-cell organisms, like amoebas.

ROY: Well, I can't see any amoeba-based cards here. Er, one moment. (SHOUTS) Margaret? Margaret? Do we have any cards with single-cell organisms on them?

MR MANN: (PROMPTING) Like amoebas.

ROY: (SHOUTS) Like amoebas?

MARGARET: I don't think so, no.

ROY: She says she doesn't think so, no.

MR MANN: Oh.

ROY: (SHOUTS) Oh. (TO MR MANN) Well, I don't know what to suggest.

MR MANN: Oh, he loves the sea...

ROY QUICKLY HOLDS UP A CARD WITH A BOAT ON IT.

MR MANN: . . . word.

Well, I can't see any amoeba-based cards here, er, one moment . . MARGARET? MARGARET? Do we have any cards with single-cell organisms on them?

ROY: Well, I can assure you we don't have anything with that on it.

MR MANN: Don't worry, I can write that in myself. Do you have any cards that just say 'Happy Sixty-Fifth Birthday . . .

ROY HOLDS UP A PLAIN 65TH-BIRTHDAY CARD.

MR MANN: . . . Michael Philipedes'?

ROY: No.

MR MANN: *Mike* Philipedes?

BAD NEWS 1

EXT: ORDINARY STREET OF TERRACED HOUSES. A POLICE CAR CONTAINING TWO POLICEMEN PULLS UP AND PARKS OUTSIDE ONE OF THE HOUSES.

TOM V/O: In Grope, PCs Bryce and Rawlinson have some sad news to impart.

INT: FRONT ROOM OF A HOUSE. PCS BRYCE AND RAWLINSON ARE ON ONE SOFA, OPPOSITE AN ANXIOUS-LOOKING MIDDLE-AGED WOMAN.

PC RAWLINSON: (SOFTLY AND SENSITIVELY) Mrs Harris, there's been an accident. I'm afraid your husband was killed in a car crash this morning.

MRS HARRIS: (SHOCKED AND UPSET) No.

PC RAWLINSON: I'm terribly sorry.

MRS HARRIS: No.

PC BRYCE: He was involved in a collision with a heavy goods vehicle.

MRS HARRIS: Oh no.

PC BRYCE: Paramedics were called, but Ken was pronounced dead at the scene.

THERE IS A PAUSE. EVENTUALLY, MRS HARRIS LOOKS UP, PUZZLED.

MRS HARRIS: Ken?

PC RAWLINSON: Yes, I'm afraid so.

MRS HARRIS: But my husband's Jonathan, Jonathan Harris.

THE CONSTABLES LOOK AT EACH OTHER, THEN CHECK THEIR NOTEBOOKS.

PC BRYCE: It was a black Ford Mondeo, Registration K5 . . .

MRS HARRIS: No, no, we only have a Fiesta.

PC RAWLINSON: We must have got the wrong house.

BOTH PCS BURST OUT LAUGHING.

PC BRYCE: (LAUGHING) Oh, I don't believe it!

MRS HARRIS: You want the other Mrs Harris, three doors down.

CONTINUING TO CHUCKLE AT THE MISUNDERSTANDING, PC BRYCE AND PC RAWLINSON GET UP FROM THE SOFA AND MAKE TO LEAVE.

PC RAWLINSON: Oh, you couldn't make it up!

PC BRYCE: Excuse us.

DENNIS WATERMAN — NEVER MIND THE BUZZCOCKS

INT: OFFICE. JEREMY RENT IS ON THE PHONE.

TOM V/O: In Troot, Jeremy Rent has just clinched another major deal for one of his clients.

JEREMY: Lovely, so there's Colin Baker to open your church fete this Saturday at two. Ooh, I can throw in Bonnie Langford for an extra ten pounds. (PAUSE) No? Please yourself, bye bye.

Lovely, so
there's
Colin
Baker to
open your
church
fete this
Saturday at
two. Ooh, I
can throw
in Bonnie
Langford
for an
extra ten
pounds.
No? Please
yourself,
bye bye.

EPISODE *three*

JEREMY PUTS THE PHONE DOWN.

VOICE ON INTERCOM: Dennis Waterman here to see you.

JEREMY: Oh lovely, send him in.

DENNIS: (OUT OF VISION, TO THE RECEPTIONIST) I'll take it for him.

DENNIS APPEARS IN THE DOORWAY, CARRYING AN ENORMOUS CUP OF TEA.

JEREMY: Hello Dennis, ooh, careful.

DENNIS: It's alright, I've got it.

DENNIS HANDS THE HUGE TEA TO JEREMY, WHOM WE SEE IN TURN TAKING A TINY CUP AND SAUCER.

JEREMY: Now you know they're showing *Minder* again on UK Gold . . .

DENNIS: (EXCITED) Oh yes?

JEREMY: Your repeat fee money came through.

JEREMY HANDS DENNIS A 50P PIECE, WHICH TO DENNIS IS HUGE.

DENNIS: Ooh, thank you.

JEREMY: And there's been lots of interest in you. In fact, the BBC just rang and they'd like you to be a guest on *Never Mind the Buzzcocks*.

DENNIS: Oh brilliant, it's my favourite; I love the bit where Phil Jupitus spontaneously gets up on the desk every week.

JEREMY: No . . . *So,* they've offered fifty pounds but I think I can get them up to fifty-five.

DENNIS: Oh, I forgot your biscuit.

JEREMY: Oh don't worry about that.

DENNIS: I insist.

DENNIS EXITS.

JEREMY: I'm trying to cut down but I . . .

DENNIS ROLLS IN AN OVERSIZED DIGESTIVE BISCUIT AND GIVES IT TO JEREMY, TO WHOM THE BISCUIT IS A NORMAL SIZE.

JEREMY: So the *Buzzcocks.* Would you like to do it?

DENNIS: So they want me to be on the panel, write the feem toon, sing the feem toon . . .

JEREMY: Well no, they've already got a theme tune, they'd just like you to be on the panel. (DENNIS'S FACE FALLS IN DISAPPOINTMENT) Fifty-five pounds, Dennis.

DENNIS: (SINGING) The show is called *Never mind the Buzzcocks* do do do do. It's hosted by the comedian and broadcaster Mark Lamar, do do do do do. Phil Jupitus is a team captain, so is Bill Bailey, he took over from Sean Hughes.

JEREMY: I'll tell them you're busy.

DENNIS: Yeah . . . OH Jeremy, there's a mouse in here!

WE SEE A TINY, REAL MOUSE WALKING ALONG THE DESK.

JEREMY: Oh he's back again is he, don't worry he'll soon scuttle out.

DENNIS STANDS ON HIS CHAIR IN FRIGHT, AND WE SEE A MAN IN A MOUSE COSTUME WALK CALMLY BEHIND DENNIS AND OUT OF THE DOOR.

BAD NEWS 2

EXT: STREET OF TERRACED HOUSES. WE SEE THE TWO POLICE OFFICERS FROM THE EARLIER SKETCH GETTING INTO THEIR POLICE CAR, PULLING OUT, AND DRIVING THREE DOORS DOWN BEFORE PARKING AGAIN.

TOM V/O: In Grope, PCs Bryce and Rawlinson *still* have some sad news to impart.

INT: LIVING ROOM. PC RAWLINSON AND PC BRYCE ARE TALKING TO ANOTHER MRS HARRIS . . .

PC RAWLINSON: (SOFTLY) We have some bad news. There's been an accident. I'm afraid your husband, *Ken* Harris, was killed in a car crash this morning.

MRS HARRIS: No, no God, no, *please*.

PC BRYCE: We're . . . terribly sorry.

Funny thing, actually . . .

Queer basher.

I'm afraid your husband, *Ken* Harris, was killed in a car crash this morning.

MRS HARRIS: No, no God, no, *please*.

PC BRYCE: We're . . . terribly sorry.

MRS HARRIS: Ken's *dead*?

PC RAWLINSON: I'm afraid so, madam.

PC BRYCE: His *black Ford Mondeo* was involved in a collision with a heavy goods vehicle. Paramedics were called, but Ken was pronounced dead at the scene.

WE FOCUS ON THE FACE OF THE DISTRAUGHT WOMAN, TEARS ROLLING DOWN HER CHEEKS AS SHE DIGESTS THE NEWS.

PC RAWLINSON: (LOOKING TO PC BRYCE, UNABLE TO STOP HIMSELF FROM SMIRKING) Funny thing, actually . . .

DAFFYD — COMING OUT 2

EXT: THE VILLAGE CHURCHYARD. DAFFYD EMERGES FROM THE CHURCH DRESSED IN FULL ELIZABETHAN 'HAMLET' COSTUME.

TOM V/O: After an audition for the local amateur production of Hamlet, the littlest homo Daffyd Thomas is off to the pub.

DAFFYD WALKS PAST AN ALTAR BOY.

ALTAR BOY: Afternoon, Daffyd!

DAFFYD: Queer basher.

INT: PUB. DAFFYD ENTERS AND SITS AT THE BAR TO ORDER.

I'm sorry, but I cannot think of a single gay actor.

DAFFYD: Bacardi and Coke please, Myfanwy

MYFANWY: Coming right up.

SHE TURNS AWAY TO MAKE HIS DRINK.

MYFANWY: So, how did the audition go?

DAFFYD: It was a complete waste of time, the director said he couldn't see me as Hamlet. I'm sorry Myfanwy, but the Llandewi Breffi Amateur Dramatics Society is completely homophobist.

MYFANWY: Oh well, what audition speech did you do?

DAFFYD: *It's Raining Men* by the Weather Girls.

MYFANWY: Well, maybe you'll get a part in the panto.

DAFFYD: I very much doubt it, Myfanwy, it's very difficult for gay people to make it in the theatre. I'm sorry, but I cannot think of a single gay actor.

THERE IS A PAUSE AS MYFANWY THINKS ABOUT THIS, UNCONVINCED.

What . . .you're gay? I had no ide

MYFANWY: Ooh, I nearly forgot, your brother rang.

DAFFYD: Really?

MYFANWY: He said he's gonna pop over, says he's got something important to tell your ma and da and he wants your advice.

DAFFYD: Oh, I wonder what it could be. I hope he hasn't got some girl pregnant.

SUDDENLY, DAFFYD'S BROTHER DEWI ENTERS THE PUB. HE IS THE SPITTING IMAGE OF DAFFYD, SIMILARLY DRESSED IN TOO-TIGHT LYCRA SHORTS AND LYCRA VEST. HE IS ACCOMPANIED BY PEDRO, A TALL MAN IN GARISH DRAG.

DAFFYD: Hello, Dewi – oh, he's bought his friend Pedro, hello.

PEDRO KISSES DAFFYD LAVISHLY AND WALKS OVER TO BAR.

PEDRO: (VERY CAMP VOICE) ¡Hola! Dos Bacardi and Coke, por favor.

DAFFYD WIPES HIS CHEEK AND TURNS TO TALK TO HIS BROTHER.

DAFFYD: So. Dewi, what's the matter?

DEWI: (CLEARLY NERVOUS) Erm, well, erm . . .

PEDRO: Ooh 'nancy boy' . . .

DEWI: You know I've always looked up to you as an older brother and, well, I'm thinking of coming out to Ma and Da and I wanted your advice.

DAFFYD: Alright, sorry, coming out as what?

DEWI: Well . . . as gay.

DAFFYD: (SHOCKED) What . . . you're gay? I had no idea!

THE CAMERA STAYS ON DEWI, IN HIS EXTRAORDINARILY CAMP LYCRA OUTFIT.

DEWI: I suppose I've hidden it quite well.

DAFFYD: Have you told Pedro?

PEDRO: (BENDING OVER AND POINTING TO HIS BACKSIDE EXCITEDLY) Si, si polla dolla coolo!

DEWI: Pedro knows.

DAFFYD: Well whatever you do, you mustn't tell Ma and Da.

DEWI: Why not?

EPISODE *three*

Pedro's gay too?!

DAFFYD: We've only got one gay in this family, we don't need two.

DEWI: But they need to know.

DAFFYD: Alright, let me think, er, how do you feel about being bisexual?

PEDRO MAKES A SOUR FACE AND MIMES PLAYING WITH A PAIR OF BREASTS WHILE THEY TALK.

DEWI: But I'm not, I'm gay.

PEDRO: Hey bisexual oh oh . . . horrible!

DAFFYD: Couldn't you at least try it?

MYFANWY: The boy likes cock, Daffyd. Look at him, he's bloody gagging for it.

AS PEDRO COUNTS, HE QUICKLY MIMES TAKING HOLD OF FOUR PENIS OUT OF THE AIR, HOLDING THEM TO HIS FACE AND SQUEEZING HIS EYES SHUT TIGHT. HE THEN MIMES WIPING HIS EYES CLEAN, AND LAUGHS MANIACALLY.

PEDRO: Sí señora. Uno, dos, tres, cuatro . . .

DAFFYD: I'm sorry Myfanwy, I am not having a gay brother, and that's that.

MYFANWY: Oh, he was like this when I told him about my first taste of fanny.

DEWI: Well I'm sorry you feel that way, Daffyd, but I'm off home to tell them now, come along Pedro.

PEDRO: (BENDING OVER AND POINTING TO HIS OWN BACKSIDE AGAIN, HOPEFULLY) Er... sexo?

DEWI: Later.

THEY LEAVE.

MYFANWY: Daffyd Thomas, that was no way to speak to your brother and his boyfriend.

DAFFYD: (SHOCKED) Pedro's gay too?!

LOU AND ANDY – CAR PARK

EXT: LOU IS WHEELING ANDY THROUGH A SUPERMARKET CAR PARK.

TOM V/O: At this supermarket in Herby, Lou has spent all of his Job Seekers allowance on food for Andy.

ANDY: You forgot the Monster Munch.

LOU: No, we've got plenty of those at home.

ANDY: Yeah, I know.

AS THEY REACH THEIR VAN, WE REVEAL THAT A CAR IS PARKED RIGHT IN FRONT OF IT, BLOCKING THEIR EXIT.

LOU: Oh no. Look what some silly arse has done. I can't get the van out now. Oh, well you wait here, I'll see if I can find someone. Oh, what a kerfuffle.

ANDY: I'm gonna miss *My Hero*.

LOU: Well there's not a lot I can do, I'll be as quick as I can.

ANDY: *My Hero!*

AS SOON AS LOU LEAVES, ANDY STEPS OUT OF HIS WHEELCHAIR, SQUATS DOWN AND BEGINS TO LIFT THE OFFENDING CAR UP WITH HIS BARE HANDS. AS THE CAR ROLLS OVER AND OUT OF THE WAY, LOU COMES INTO VIEW WITH THE CAR PARK ATTENDANT. UNSEEN TO LOU, ANDY SITS BACK IN HIS WHEELCHAIR.

LOU LOOKS AT THE ROLLED-OVER CAR, AND TURNS TO THE ATTENDANT.

LOU: Alright, I don't think we need you any more . . .

LOU TRIES TO MANOEUVRE ANDY INTO HIS VAN.

BY DAFFYD THOMAS

LLANDEWI BREFFI

♦ A Visitor's Guide ♦

PRODUCED BY LLANDEWI BREFFI
PARISH COUNCIL
✝

FARM - Very homophobist. Not one single gay cow.

FARM

POST OFFICE - Despite having Queen's head on stamps, not gay-friendly. Good place to cash giro, though.

DOCTOR'S SURGERY - As an out gay man, the doctor always gives me free condoms. I now have over one hundred and fifty at home.

HAIRDRESSERS - Hairdressers are notoriously heterosexual and this fella - Han 'Fanny' Rhys - is no exception. However, with the nearest rival over half a mile away I am forced to have my hair cut here. (Incidentally, my own hairstyle is known as a 'Bronski Beat-era Somerville').

POST OFFICE

HAIRDRESSER

DOCTOR

'SCARCROW AND MRS' KING' PUB -

A no-go area for gays despite presence of dirty lezzer Myfanwy behind bar. Best Bacardi and coke this side of Bangor.

PUB

NEWSAGENT -
Very heterosexist selection of magazines on sale. Apart from Gay Times, Attitude, Axm, Pride, Pink Paper, Boyz, Powerballin', Unzipped, CuteAss, Freshmeat and Cock Monthly, there are no gay titles on display.

LIBRARY -
Have recently installed a gay section which I'm very much hoping will be burnt by the many homophobes in the village. If not, I will be obliged to do it myself.

VILLAGE GREEN -
Would make an excellent cruising zone were it not for the fact that I am the only gay in the village.

LLANDEWI BREFFI JUNIOR SCHOOL
- Despite my campaign and petition signed by Stephen Gately, David Furnish and that guy from 'Gimme Gimme', Gay Studies still does not appear on the syllabus.

EPISODE *four*

TOM V/O: Britain, Britain, Britain. Recently awarded the O.B.E., but why? Not just because we won all those wars or invented the scone, no, it's because of the people of Britain, the British, the Brits, or 'scum' as we are affectionately known around the world. Let's take a trip around this fragrant isle and find out just who are them and what are their doings – bring it on.

VICKY POLLARD — POLICE STATION

EXT: POLICE STATION. WE SEE VICKY'S GANG STOP A YOUNG POLICEMAN WHO IS ABOUT TO ENTER THE STATION. TWO OF THE GIRLS CHAT TO HIM, WHILE THE THIRD STEALS HIS WALLET.

TOM V/O: The police, or 'pigs' as they are affectionately known, are always busy solving crimes. Popular crimes include armed robbery, GBH and my personal favourite, murder.

INT: POLICE STATION. A POLICEWOMAN STANDS IN THE DOORWAY OF AN OFFICE, USHERING VICKY OUT.

POLICE OFFICER: Perhaps the next time you try to steal a horse, you'll think again. Don't tut, I'm letting you off with a warning this time, think yourself lucky.

VICKY: Alright! What do you think you are, the law or summit?

AS VICKY WALKS OUT OF THE POLICE STATION, SHE SEES A POSTER OFFERING A REWARD OF £10,000 FOR INFORMATION ON A ROBBERY.

VICKY: (READING, AWESTRUCK) Ten hundred thousand pounds . . .

INT: INTERVIEW ROOM. TWO POLICE OFFICERS SHOW VICKY TO A SEAT.

POLICE OFFICER: Now Vicky, you say you witnessed the robbery?

VICKY: No but yeah but no because what happened was was this whole robbery happened because this bloke robbed this bank or something

POLICE OFFICER: It was a jeweller's . . .

VICKY: Oh yeah it was a jeweller's and I saw the man who's done it and he was like so guilty and it was like so obviously him and I done a drawing of him and he looked exactly like that (HOLDS UP A CHILDISH SCRIBBLE), please can I have ten hundred thousand pounds now please?

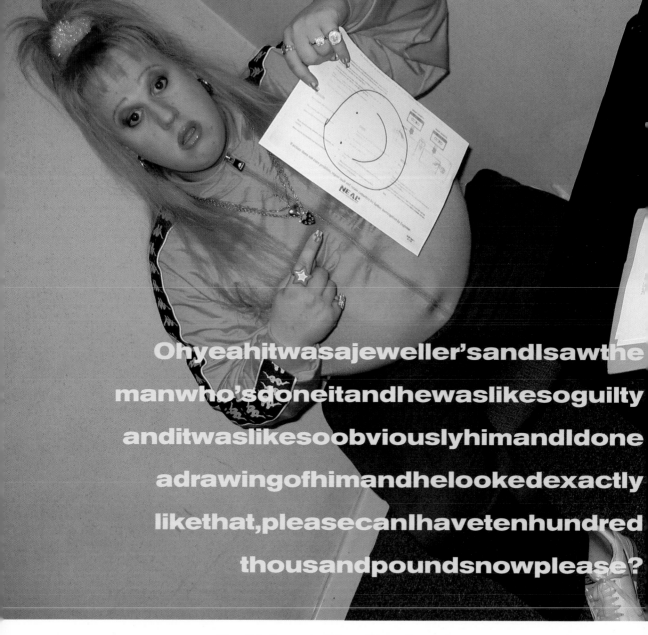

Ohyeahitwasajeweller'sandIsawthe
manwho'sdoneitandhewaslikesoguilty
anditwaslikesoobviouslyhimandIdone
adrawingofhimandhelookedexactly
likethat,pleasecanIhavetenhundred
thousandpoundsnowplease?

POLICE OFFICER: (WEARILY) You didn't see anything, did you?

VICKY: Oh my God I so can't believe you just said that I was right in the middle of it and he tried to nick my brand-new Reebok trainers as well so I well reckon I should get consemption for that as well.

POLICE OFFICER: You do know it's an offence to waste police time?

VICKY: No but yeah but no but yeah but no but yeah but no because I'm not wasting police time because you know Misha well she saw the whole thing right because she was bunking off school because she was gonna go down the Wimpy and get off with Luke Griffiths only she never because he's been trying to grow a moustache but it just looks like pubes she got off with Luke Talbot instead only don't tell Bethany that because she's fancied Luke Talbot ever since she flashed her fanny at him during Home Ec.

POLICE OFFICER: I can't see what this has got to do with the investigation?

VICKY: I'm getting there. So anyway this whole other thing happened because Ellie Barnes who everyone knows is a total slagbag has been completely going around saying that Craig Wilson's brother left a rubber Johnny on Miss Turner's desk.

POLICE OFFICER: Vicky, we're just interested in the robbery.

VICKY: What robbery I never done no robbery. Oh my God this is like the time Samina Geshwani said that I threw a tampon at Ian Buchan during assembly which she was well out of order to say that because I would so never do that. It was a panty pad.

THE POLICE OFFICER BEGINS TO WALK TOWARDS THE DOOR.

POLICE OFFICER: You have no idea who committed this crime, do you?

VICKY STANDS UP.

EPISODE

Oh my God did you see that, she well just gave me guiltys.

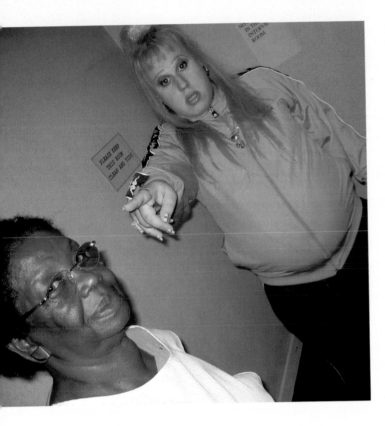

VICKY: Oh my God I so can't believe you just said that I was well just about to tell you who like the whole robber was and everything.

THE POLICE OFFICERS MAKE TO LEAVE, AND WE SEE A FRIENDLY-LOOKING CLEANER STANDING OUTSIDE THE OFFICE.

CLEANER: Are you all finished in here?

POLICE OFFICER: Yeah.

VICKY THINKS FOR A SECOND, AND THEN POINTS AT THE CLEANING LADY.

VICKY: She done it.

THE CLEANING LADY LOOKS BEMUSED.

VICKY: Oh my God did you see that, she well just gave me guiltys.

MAGGIE AND JUDY — MINCE PIES

INT: A FESTIVE CHURCH GATHERING. WE SEE ALTARS BOYS HAPPILY TAKING MINCE PIES FROM THE CHOIR MASTER.

TOM V/O: The people of Pox are enjoying light refreshments after their annual carol service. I love carols, though I do prefer Barbara's.

MAGGIE AND JUDY ARE TALKING TO THE VICAR.

MAGGIE: Lovely service, Vicar.

JUDY: Yes, Vicar.

VICAR: Thank you, ladies.

MAGGIE: To hear the children sing all those carols: for me, that is the true meaning of Christmas.

THE CHOIR MASTER WALKS UP TO THEM WITH A TRAY OF MINCE PIES.

VICAR: Yes they did do well, didn't they, but it's all down to the choir master.

CHOIR MASTER: Oh thank you, Vicar. Er, mince pie, ladies?

MAGGIE: (LAUGHING MERRILY) Oh thank you. Ooh, they're still hot!

MAGGIE: Mmm lovely, did you make these?

VICAR: Yes, with my partner Steven.

MAGGIE BEGINS TO HEAVE, WHILE JUDY LOOKS AT HER ANXIOUSLY, KNOWING WHAT'S ABOUT TO HAPPEN. MAGGIE PROJECTILE VOMITS ALL OVER THE CHOIR MASTER, AND THEN STOPS. SHE TURNS TO THE VICAR AND VOMITS ALL OVER HIM, AND PAUSES AGAIN. FINALLY, SHE THROWS UP ALL OVER JUDY.

THERE IS A PAUSE.

MAGGIE: (CONVERSATIONALLY) By the way, I thought the solo in 'Silent Night' was divine.

THE CHOIR MASTER AND VICAR ARE LEFT STANDING THERE COVERED IN VOMIT, STUNNED. MAGGIE POPS A MINCE PIE BACK ON THE TRAY.

CHOIR MASTER: Thank you.

Planning a wank?

NOSY NEWSAGENT

EXT: CAMERA PANNING ROUND A HIGH STREET. WE SEE A NEWSAGENT PUTTING UP A HANDWRITTEN SIGN IN HIS SHOP WINDOW WHICH SAYS 'ONLY 200 SCHOOLCHILDREN AT A TIME'.

TOM V/O: It's five to Jackie S, not Jackie P, and in the northern town of Dirty Boy lies this sublime newsagent's.

INT: NEWSAGENT'S. A CUSTOMER ENTERS AND BEGINS TO BROWSE.

SHOPKEEPER: Hello.

AS THE CUSTOMER LOOKS AROUND THE SHOP, THE SHOPKEEPER, WHO IS A LITTLE TOO EAGER TO HELP, ATTEMPTS TO SECOND-GUESS HIS CHOICES.-

THE CUSTOMER OPENS THE CANNED-DRINK FRIDGE.

SHOPKEEPER: (SMILING) Thirsty?

THE CUSTOMER LOOKS A LITTLE EMBARRASSED, AND TURNS TO LOOK AT THE CHOCOLATE BARS.

SHOPKEEPER: Hungry?

EMBARRASSED, THE CUSTOMER MAKES HIS WAY OVER TO THE SHELF OF NEWSPAPERS.

SHOPKEEPER: (STILL SMILING) Looking to catch up on the day's news and sport?

THE CUSTOMER BEGINS TO PICK UP A NOTEBOOK.

SHOPKEEPER: Hoping to write letter to friend or relative?

THE CUSTOMER'S EYES GO UP TO THE TOP SHELF OF MAGAZINES. WE SEE THE SHOPKEEPER, STILL SMILING, WEIGHING UP WHETHER TO SAY SOMETHING. THE CUSTOMER LOOKS AT HIM, WAITING FOR HIM TO SPEAK. FINALLY, THE SHOPKEEPER CAN'T STOP HIMSELF.

SHOPKEEPER: Planning a wank?

THE CUSTOMER DECIDES AGAINST TAKING SOMETHING FROM THE TOP SHELF, AND PUTS A DRINK AND NEWSPAPER ON THE COUNTER.

CUSTOMER: (AVOIDING EYE CONTACT) Just these . . .

MAN IN RESTAURANT 1

INT: RESTAURANT. WE SEE A GENTLEMAN SITTING, ALONE, AT A TABLE. A WAITER COMES OVER.

WAITER: Can I take your order, sir?

MAN: Yes, I'll have the foie gras to start.

WAITER: And for your main course, sir?

MAN: Poached guinea fowl.

WAITER: Would you like vegetables with that, sir?

MAN: Just dauphinoise potatoes.

WAITER: *Excellent* choice, sir.

THERE IS A PAUSE.

MAN: And a Double Decker.

THE WAITER NODS AND LEAVES.

**And a
Double Decker.**

EMILY AND FLORENCE – THE BALLET

EXT: A RATHER GRAND-LOOKING THEATRE.

TOM V/O: Today, Emily is taking Florence to the ballet.

EMILY AND FLORENCE APPEAR WEARING TUTUS, AND MAKE THEIR WAY TOWARDS THE THEATRE.

FLORENCE: Emily, you're absolutely sure this is what ladies wear when they go down the ballet?

EMILY: Trust me, my dear Florence, all the best ladies dress like this. Now just do as I do and no one will suspect a thing (LAUGHS EXCITEDLY) ooh!

TOM V/O: I love to slip into a tu tu. Bishop Desmond Tu Tu.

INT: THEATRE LOBBY. FLORENCE AND EMILY DANCE THEIR WAY TOWARDS THE TICKET COUNTER.

FLORENCE: Good evening, two ladies' tickets for the ballet, s'il vous plaît.

TICKET SELLER: They're all the same price, sir, where would you like to sit?

FLORENCE: Er, er, in a seat, please.

EMILY: Er, yes, facing the stage, we love the ballet you see.

FLORENCE: Yes, we're just two ladies who love the ballet!

EMILY: Florence here was very nearly a ballerina herself, weren't you?

FLORENCE: (SMILES) Yes. (TURNS TO EMILY, PUZZLED) Was I?

EMILY: Yes, she always dreamed of being a prima ballerina.

FLORENCE: Oh yes, but then I became a hod carrier.

EMILY: I am definitely a lady and I have been coming to the ballet now for many a year, I've seen all the finest companies, the Rambert, the Bolshoi . . .

FLORENCE: Legs and Co...

TICKET SELLER: That's two tickets in the stalls at fifty pounds each, how would you like to pay?

EMILY LOOKS THROUGH HER WALLET, AND PULLS OUT A CARD.

EMILY: Erm . . . Switch.

TICKET SELLER: (READING THE CARD) 'Mr Edward Howard'.

EMILY: (EMBARRASSED LAUGHTER) My husband's card, silly me.

Yes, she always dreamed of being a prima ballerina.

Oh yes, but then I became a hod carrier.

EMILY MIMES 'MONEY' WITH HER THUMB AND FOREFINGER TO FLORENCE.

EMILY: Do you have any cash, Florence my dear?

EMILY: (RELUCTANTLY) One moment, I should have some in here somewhere, er, where are we. Oh yes (HANDING THE MONEY OVER TO THE TICKET SELLER) twenty, forty, sixty (IN A MAN'S VOICE) eighty, a ton.

EMILY: Merci beaucoup.

FLORENCE: Excuse me, where's the bogs?

EMILY CORRECTS HIM IN AN APPROPRIATELY LADYLIKE FASHION.

EMILY: Où est les chambres . . . de pee-pee?

TICKET SELLER: The toilets are through there, but the performance is about to start.

FLORENCE: Ta very much.

INT: MEN'S TOILETS. TWO MEN ARE STANDING AT THE URINALS. EMILY AND FLORENCE ENTER, SKIPPING AND DANCING, AND STAND AT THE URINALS THEMSELVES.

EMILY: Two ladies, having a pee.

FLORENCE: Pay no heed.

FLORENCE CAN'T HELP DANCING AND TWIRLING AS SHE PEES. IN DOING SO, SHE SPLASHES ALL OVER BOTH OF THE MEN STANDING EITHER SIDE OF HER.

FLORENCE: Oh, whoops a daisy.

LOU AND ANDY — THE BABY JESUS

EXT: HOUSING ESTATE. LOU IS MAKING HIS WAY UP TO HIS HOUSE, CARRYING CHRISTMAS DECORATIONS. SPOTTING A SLIGHTLY CRUSHED CAN OF BEER ON TOP OF A WALL, HE LOOKS AROUND, PICKS THE CAN UP FURTIVELY AND TAKES A DRINK. ALMOST IMMEDIATELY HE GAGS, AND PULLS A SODDEN CIGARETTE OUT OF HIS MOUTH.

TOM V/O: Christmas was first celebrated in Britain in 1986 to commemorate the birth of Lord Martin Christmas.

INT: LIVING ROOM. ANDY IS SITTING AT THE TABLE, ENGROSSED IN THE TV. WITHOUT LOOKING, HE POURS A WHOLE PINT OF MILK INTO THE BOX OF CEREAL HE'S HOLDING, AND BEGINS TO EAT STRAIGHT FROM THE BOX WITH A SPOON.

LOU IS BEHIND HIM, GETTING READY TO DO THE IRONING.

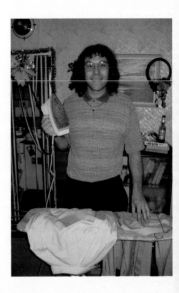

Où est les chambres . . . de pee-pee?

I want to
go
dressed
as the
Baby
Jesus.

BABY JESUS

And so it came to pass that Mary and Joseph made their way to the city of Bethlehem. They sought high and low for refuge, but there was no room at the inn. I LOOK A PILLOCK

LOU: Does that mean you're gonna be windy in church today?

ANDY: Yeah, I know.

LOU: What do you want to wear, 'cause I'm gonna put the iron on?

ANDY: Baby Jesus.

LOU: What about the Baby Jesus?

ANDY: I want to go dressed as the Baby Jesus.

LOU: Mmm, I'm not really sure that's a good idea, I know you *like* the Baby Jesus . . .

ANDY: I *love* the Baby Jesus.

LOU: I'm not sure with you dressing up as him is gonna go down that well in church . . . it's gonna be a right kerfuffle making you up a Baby Jesus outfit at such short notice.

ANDY: (FIRMLY) Baby Jesus.

LOU: My sweet Lord.

INT: CHURCH. THE VICAR IS ADDRESSING THE CONGREGATION.

VICAR: And now, Andrew Pipkin is going to read for us from the Gospel according to Saint Matthew. Andrew . . .

LOU PUSHES ANDY TO THE STAGE IN HIS WHEELCHAIR. HE IS DRESSED AS THE BABY JESUS, WITH A CARDBOARD BOX FULL OF STRAW STUCK TO HIS BACK. HE BEGINS TO READ FROM THE BIBLE.

ANDY: And so it came to pass that Mary and Joseph made their way to the city of Bethlehem. They sought high and low for refuge, but there was no room at the inn. I look a pillock.

DR LAWRENCE AND ANNE – THEATRE

INT: THEATRE. DR BEAGRIE AND DR LAWRENCE ARE WATCHING THE PLAY.

TOM V/O: In Kidney, Dr Lawrence has taken Dr Beagrie along to see one of his patients take part in an amateur production of The Importance of Being Earnest.

ACTOR 1: 'Ah, but you must be serious. I hate people who are not serious about meals.'

DR LAWRENCE: (WHISPERING TO DR BEAGRIE) Such a funny play, isn't it. I know Anne's worked very hard on it, I think she's going to be fantastic.

ACTOR 2: (INTRODUCING A NEW ARRIVAL ON STAGE) 'Lady Bracknell.'

DR LAWRENCE: (WHISPERING) Oh, this will be her now.

ACTOR 3: 'Good afternoon, Lady Bracknell.'

I'd love to see her do some Shakespeare.

ANNE COMES ONTO THE STAGE, WEARING A LATE-VICTORIAN DRESS.

ANNE: Eh eh eh!

ACTOR 1: 'May I offer you a cucumber sandwich?'

ANNE LOOKS DOWN AT THE SANDWICHES, SQUAWKS AND BATS THEM OUT OF THE MAN'S HANDS, INTO THE AUDIENCE.

ANNE: Eh eh eh!

DR LAWRENCE: (WHISPERS) Oh, the handbag line's coming up, I'm dying to see how she does it.

ACTOR 3: 'I was just telling Algernon how I was found in the cloakroom at Victoria Station, in a handbag.'

ANNE: Eh eh eh?

DR LAWRENCE: (TO DR BEAGRIE) *Brilliant!*

ACTOR 3: (SOLDIERING ON) 'Erm, yes Lady Bracknell, I was in a handbag, a somewhat large black leather handbag with handles on it.'

ANNE BENDS DOWN AND OVERTURNS A TABLE, SQUAWKING.

ANNE: Eh eh eh!

ACTOR 3: 'I was in the cloakroom at Victoria Station.'

ACTOR 1: 'Ah, the Brighton line.'

ANNE WALKS OVER TO THE THIRD ACTOR AND SLOWLY AND ALLURINGLY LIFTS HER SKIRT UP IN FRONT OF HIM.

ACTOR 3: (FLUSTERED) 'Yes, I need . . .'

DR LAWRENCE: (WHISPERING, PUZZLED) I don't remember this bit.

(THE CURTAINS BEGIN TO CLOSE AS ANNE CLOSES IN ON THE SEATED ACTOR, BEGINNING TO HOLD HER SKIRT OVER HIM)

DR LAWRENCE: I'd love to see her do some Shakespeare.

ANNE: (AS THE CURTAINS CLOSE) Eh eh eh!

MARJORIE DAWES/FATFIGHTERS —
CHRISTMAS MEAL OUT

INT: RESTAURANT. THE CAMERA PANS ACROSS A BUSY RESTAURANT DECKED IN CHRISTMAS DECORATIONS. WE SEE A
WAITRESS MAKING HER WAY OVER TO THE FATFIGHTERS MEMBERS AND MARJORIE, WHO ARE ALL SITTING ROUND A
TABLE WAITING TO BE SERVED.

TOM V/O: Every Christmas, Marjorie Dawes takes her FatFighters group out for a
meal. The best meal I ever had was in Rome, off the beaten track in a little back
street: Chicken McNuggets and chips.

MARJORIE: I asked for a corner table because I don't really think it's fair on the other
diners to have to watch fat people eat.

PAT: It looks nice, doesn't it, I don't know what to have.

MARJORIE: Now, it's Christmas, so everyone can order what they like, yeah, you've got to have a night off ain't ya, eh, we're not FatFighters now, are we? (LAUGHS AND TURNS TO MEERA) I'm not sure they do curry here Moira, but why don't you order some English food, yeah, spag bol?

WAITRESS: Well, is everyone ready?

MARJORIE: Er, I think so. (BRIGHTLY) Er, by the way we're all from FatFighters, aren't we, gang!

ALL: Yeah.

MARJORIE: In case you're wondering what I'm doing with them, I'm the group leader.

WAITRESS: Yes, what would you like?

TANIA: I think I'll have the garlic bread to start.

MARJORIE: Oh I don't think you should be having a starter, Tania, do you?

TANIA: Oh OK then, in that case I'll just have the Chicken Kiev.

WAITRESS: Anything on the side?

MARJORIE: No.

PAUL: I'll have the steak and chips, please.

MARJORIE: No, just give him a salad without the dressing.

MEERA: Can I have lasagne?

MARJORIE: What I think is best, Moira, is if you just point at what you want.

MARJORIE: Alright Pat, your turn.

PAT: Well, seeing as you're ordering for us, I might as well just have a salad.

MARJORIE: Cancel that, do you have any dust? A little bit of dust? No? Dust? No? Dust? Little bit of dust? No? Dust? Little bit? No? . . .

(MARJORIE CONTINUES IN THIS FASHION FOR SEVERAL SECONDS, REPEATING HERSELF MORE AND MORE QUICKLY)

WAITRESS: No.

MARJORIE: Well in that case just give her a glass of water.

WAITRESS: Anything for you?

MARJORIE: Oh no, nothing for me, thanks, I want to keep my figure, I never eat after six.

PAUL: (CHANGING THE SUBJECT) So, has everyone finished their Christmas shopping, then?

MEERA: No, I haven't done any of it yet.

MARJORIE VERY DELIBERATELY DROPS HER FORK AND, WHILE THE OTHERS SPEAK, GOES UNDER THE TABLE TO FETCH IT.

MARJORIE: Oh I've just dropped my fork, 'scuse me.

WHILE THE FATFIGHTERS CONTINUE THEIR CONVERSATION, WE HEAR PIGGY EATING NOISES FROM UNDER THE TABLE. A HAND REACHES UP AND GRABS SOME BREAD, TO PAUL'S SURPRISE, AND WE HEAR MORE GOBBLING NOISES.

EVENTUALLY, MARJORIE COMES OUT FROM UNDER THE TABLE, WITH FOOD ALL OVER HER FACE.

MARJORIE: (INNOCENTLY) So, what's everyone doing for Christmas?

THE GROUP LOOK STUNNED.

DAFFYD — LIBRARY

EXT: THE RECEPTION AREA OF A LIBRARY. DAFFYD STRIDES IN CARRYING A LARGE PROTEST BOARD WHICH READS: '*GAY RIGHTS NOW*'.

TOM V/O: Over in Llandewi Breffi, lovely gay boy Daffyd Thomas is taking a stand against his local library.

DAFFYD HANDS HIS SIGN TO ONE OF THE LIBRARIANS AND KEEPS WALKING TOWARDS THE SHELVES OF BOOKS.

LIBRARIAN: Morning, Daffyd.

DAFFYD: (ALOOF) We're taking action, Mrs Jones.

LIBRARIAN: Oh right . . .

DAFFYD PROCEEDS TO SWEEP A ROW OF BOOKS OFF THE SHELVES, AND STARTS REPLACING THEM WITH BOOKS OF HIS OWN.

THE LIBRARIAN WALKS OVER TO DAFFYD, PUZZLED.

LIBRARIAN: Is there something the matter?

DAFFYD DEFIANTLY HOLDS UP SOME OF HIS BOOKS TO SHOW THE LIBRARIAN.

DAFFYD: Quentin Crisp, *The Naked Civil Servant*; the Joe Orton *Diaries*; *My Struggle*, Dale Winton . . . It's not easy being the only gay in the village, in fact it's bloody hard, books like this have been a lifeline to me.

DAFFYD HOLDS UP A BOOK: 'MICHAEL PORTILLO: I TRIED IT ONCE AND DIDN'T LIKE IT.'

> It's not easy being the only gay in the village, in fact it's bloody hard, books like this have been a lifeline to me.

WHILE THEY ARE TALKING, ANOTHER LIBRARY VISITOR REACHES OVER AND PICKS UP ONE OF DAFFYD'S BOOKS.

OLD LADY: Oh, Will Young.

DAFFYD: (CROSSLY) Put that down, it's a gay book for gays. (DAFFYD PUTS A HOME-MADE SIGN ON THE SHELF THAT READS: 'GAY (+LESBIAN INC. BISEXUAL) There we go. This library now has its own 'gay and lesbian, including bi-sexual' section. Another step forward for the Llandewi Breffi Gay Liberation Front: me!

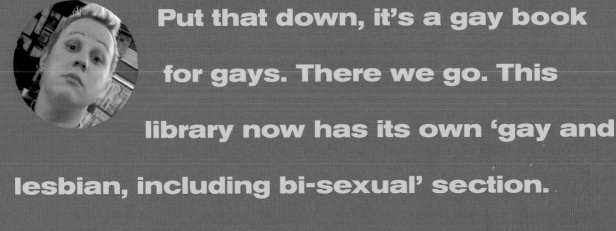

Put that down, it's a gay book for gays. There we go. This library now has its own 'gay and lesbian, including bi-sexual' section. Another step forward for the Llandewi Breffi Gay Liberation Front: **me!**

HE MAKES A PROUD FIST IN THE AIR.

LIBRARIAN: Well actually, Daffyd, I don't know whether you've ever been past travel but we do have quite a popular gay section.

DAFFYD: What?

LIBRARIAN: Come with me . . .

SHE LEADS DAFFYING THROUGH THE LIBRARY TO A SECTION FULL OF GAY MEN IN VARIOUS LEATHER AND LYCRA OUTFITS, STANDING AROUND READING.

DAFFYD: What the hell is . . .

GAY MAN: Ssh!

MAN IN RESTAURANT 2

INT: RESTAURANT. WE SEE THE SAME WAITER AS BEFORE WALKING OVER TO THE
GENTLEMAN'S TABLE.

WAITER: Have you decided what you're having yet, sir?

MAN: No.

WAITER: The oysters are very good today, sir.

MAN: Alright then, half a dozen oysters to start.

WAITER: And for your main course?

MAN: The liver . . . with baby onions
and savoy cabbage.

WAITER: Excellent choice, sir.

PAUSE.

MAN: And a Lion Bar and a Pepperami.

THE WAITER NODS AND LEAVES.

SEBASTIAN AND MICHAEL — PREGNANT

EXT: DOWNING STREET. SEBASTIAN EMERGES FROM NO. 10 AND PLACES A GARDEN GNOME ON THE DOORSTEP, NEXT
TO THE POLICEMAN WHO IS STANDING GUARD. SEBASTIAN TURNS, GOES BACK INSIDE AND CLOSES THE DOOR.

TOM V/O: This is No.10 Downing Street. Today the Prime Minister and his wife are
preparing to make an important announcement. I don't want to spoil it, but
basically they're having a baby.

INT: PRIME MINISTER'S OFFICE. A JOYFUL PRIME MINISTER AND HIS WIFE ARE ON THE SOFA, PROUDLY ADMIRING HER
BUMP.

THERE IS A KNOCK AT THE DOOR.

MICHAEL: Come.

SEBASTIAN: Morning, Prime Minister.

MICHAEL: Good morning, Sebastian, you know my wife, don't you.

WIFE: (FRIENDLY) Hello.

SEBASTIAN IS CLEARLY JEALOUS AND IN A HUFF.

SEBASTIAN: (COLDLY) Hi. Maybe I should just go?

MICHAEL: No no no, please sit down.

SEBASTIAN TAKES A SEAT OPPOSITE THE COUPLE.

MICHAEL: Actually, we have something to tell you. I'd like you to issue a press statement confirming that Sarah is pregnant.

SEBASTIAN: (IN A LOW VOICE) What?

MICHAEL'S WIFE: I'm three months gone and, well, the bump's beginning to show.

MICHAEL: Actually, you're the first person on the staff to know, it's, it's great news, isn't it.

SEBASTIAN: What*ever*. (PETULANTLY) So is that it, or is there something important you need to discuss?

MICHAEL: Well, I thought it would be quite a big story this morning and I'd like you to handle it. (THE PHONE RINGS) Oh, Chief Whip, excuse me.

SEBASTIAN AND PRIME MINISTER'S WIFE REMAIN SEATED WHILE THE PRIME MINISTER TAKES THE PHONE CALL.

SEBASTIAN: (HISSING) So it's definitely his, is it?

MICHAEL'S WIFE: (FLABBERGASTED) Yes, of course it is. Look, Sebastian, we need to compose this statement.

SEBASTIAN: (MUTTERING) Very clever . . .

MICHAEL'S WIFE: Excuse me?

SEBASTIAN: What you've done, very clever.

MICHAEL'S WIFE: I'm sorry?

SEBASTIAN: Got yourself up the duff. What, did you say you were on the pill, you tricked him into it?

MICHAEL'S WIFE: No, we've been married for twelve years, trying for children for two.

SEBASTIAN: You've worked it, girl, I give you that.

MICHAEL'S WIFE: What?

SEBASTIAN: You've got him, you've won but let me tell

You've got him, you've won but let me tell you this, **girlfriend**, while you're piling on the pounds eating for two, he's gonna be looking elsewhere.

you this, girlfriend, while you're piling on the pounds eating for two, he's gonna be looking elsewhere.

MICHAEL'S WIFE: (ANGRILY) How *dare* you.

SHE GETS UP AND STORMS OUT OF THE OFFICE. THE PRIME MINISTER HAS JUST FINISHED HIS PHONE CALL.

MICHAEL: Oh, is she alright?

SEBASTIAN: Yeah, women's problems.

MICHAEL: Erm, shall we get on with this statement.

SEBASTIAN: Yep, erm . . . 'We regret to announce?' . . . 'She's done it, the bitch has done it.' . . .

MICHAEL: (STERNLY) Explain.

SEBASTIAN: Oh sorry, Prime Minister.

SEBASTIAN GETS UP AND STANDS CLOSELY BEHIND THE SEATED PRIME MINISTER.

SEBASTIAN: (INTO THE PRIME MINISTER'S EAR, INTIMATELY) You know, we could have adopted.

SEBASTIAN WALKS OUT SEDUCTIVELY, LEAVING THE PRIME MINISTER STUNNED.

EPISODE

BANK CLERK 3

EXT: STREET. AN OLD LADY BENDS DOWN TO COLLECT HER DOG'S MESS, STANDS UP STRAIGHT – AND TOSSES IT INTO A CHARITY BUCKET BEFORE WALKING OFF.

TOM V/O: People in Britain like to keep their money safe, either by depositing into a bank or by nailing it to their front door.

INT: BANK OFFICE. BANK CLERK CAROL BEER IS OFFERING MORTGAGE ADVICE TO A YOUNG COUPLE.

MAN: It's on the market for eighty thousand, which is cheap for round here.

CAROL: Oh yes?

MAN: But the estate agent reckons we could probably get them down to seventy-five.

CAROL: (DEADPAN) Sounds great. Well, the best mortgage for you is the Mid-West First-Time Buyer Plus.

MAN: Oh yeah?

CAROL PROCEEDS TO READ FROM AN INFORMATION LEAFLET.

CAROL: Yeah. There's a fixed rate of four point nine per cent over five years and an instant cashback of ten thousand pounds.

MAN: Right.

WOMAN: (BRIGHTLY) It sounds good.

MAN: Yeah, we'll go for that, please.

CAROL TURNS TO THE COMPUTER AND TAPS SOME KEYS. THERE IS A PAUSE.

CAROL: Computer says 'No'.

SHE COUGHS AT THE COUPLE, HARD.

HARVEY AND JANE – WEDDING CATERER

INT: LIVING ROOM.

TOM V/O: This upper class family are meeting their wedding caterer. If you're not sure which class you are, simply pull back your foreskin, where you'll find the word 'lower', 'middle' or 'upper'.

WEDDING CATERER: For the starter, I was thinking of wild asparagus tips with hollandaise sauce. Of course I'm very open to suggestions, so if there's anything that you particularly like, it's your wedding, you should say.

HARVEY: Bitty.

WEDDING CATERER: Sorry?

CELIA: Not now, Harvey.

HARVEY'S GRANDMOTHER: I don't like asparagus.

CELIA: Well, maybe you could do some smoked salmon, for my mother?

HARVEY: Bitty.

CELIA: No, Harvey.

HARVEY: (INSISTENT) Bitty

CELIA: You've just had Bitty. (TURNING TO THE CATERER) Please.

WEDDING CATERER: Well . . . Erm, for the main, I was going to suggest breast of pigeon with wild mushroom risotto.

JANE: That sounds lovely.

HARVEY'S GRANDMOTHER: It sounds a bit rich.

HARVEY: I don't like risotto.

WEDDING CATERER: Well, is there anything that you'd prefer.

HARVEY: Bitty.

GERALD: Come on, Harvey.

WEDDING CATERER: We will of course offer a vegetarian option.

GERALD: Oh bloody vegetarians, string up the lot of 'em, I say.

HARVEY: (PLEADING) Bitty, bitty.

CELIA RELENTS AND BECKONS HIM OVER. HE LIES ACROSS HER LAP AND BEGINS TO BREAST-FEED, LEAVING THE CATERER STUNNED. CELIA CARRIES ON CHATTING.

CELIA: We went to a wedding in the spring and they had these wonderful roasted artichoke hearts, and a lot of people went for them over the beef Wellington.

WEDDING CATERER: (DUMBSTRUCK) Yes, that does . . . quite often happen.

CELIA: (CROSSLY, TO HARVEY) Oh, you're biting!

GERALD: Well I'm not surprised, you're a very greedy boy this morning.

HARVEY: Bitty.

WITH CELIA OUT OF MILK, HER MOTHER STEPS IN HELPFULLY . . .

HARVEY'S GRANDMOTHER: (BEGINNING TO LIFT UP HER TOP)

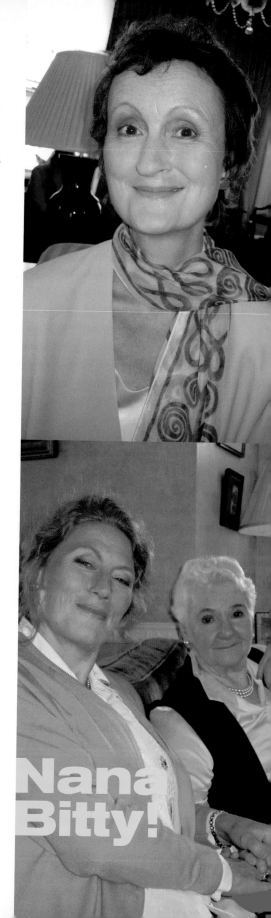

Nana Bitty!

Don't worry dear, I should have some.

HARVEY: (FACE LIGHTING UP) Nana Bitty!

HARVEY REACHES OVER SO THAT HE IS NOW LYING ACROSS HIS GRANDMOTHER'S LAP AS WELL, AND BEGINS TO
BREAST-FEED FROM HER. THE WEDDING CATERER IS SPEECHLESS.

HARVEY'S GRANDMOTHER: Any ideas on pudding?

KENNY CRAIG — CAR PARK

EXT: AERIAL SHOT OF A SUPERMARKET CAR PARK. THE CAMERA PANS DOWN TO SHOW KENNY REVERSING HIS CAR
OUT OF A PARKING SPACE, AND HITTING THE BACK CORNER OF THE CAR NEXT TO HIM IN THE PROCESS.

TOM V/O: At the supermarket in Slaughter, stage hypnotist Kenny Craig has just
finished his shopping. Supermarkets were introduced into Britain to destroy small
businesses and create a sense of social alienation.

KENNY GETS OUT OF HIS CAR AND WALKS AROUND TO SURVEY THE DAMAGE. THE ADJACENT CAR'S BUMPER IS BADLY
DAMAGED.

CAR PARK ATTENDANT: (CALLING OVER STERNLY) Excuse me.

KENNY: Yes?

CAR PARK ATTENDANT: Are you gonna leave your insurance details?

Are you gonna leave your insurance details?

KENNY: I didn't hit the car.

CAR PARK ATTENDANT: I saw you do it!

KENNY SIGHS AND TURNS TO HYPNOTIZE THE ATTENDANT.

KENNY: Look into my eyes, look into my eyes, the eyes, the eyes, not around the eyes,
don't look around the eyes, look into my eyes (CLICKS HIS FINGERS), you're under. You did
not, repeat not, see me hit that car. Three – two – one . . . (CLICK) you're back in the room.

CAR PARK ATTENDANT: (COMING TO) You didn't see who hit that car did you, mate?

A LADY WALKS OVER QUICKLY.

LADY: Yes I did, it was him.

CAR PARK ATTENDANT: No it wasn't.

LADY: (TO KENNY) Yes it was, I saw you do it!

ANNOYED, KENNY GROANS AND TURNS TO HYPNOTIZE THE LADY AS WELL.

KENNY: Look into my eyes, look into my eyes, around the eyes, don't look around the eyes, look into my eyes, (CLICKS HIS FINGERS) you're under. You did not, repeat not, see me hit that car; (TURNING BACK TO THE ATTENDANT) nor did you. Three – two – one . . .

WE NOW SEE A MAN WALKING TOWARDS THEM WITH TWO BIG BAGS OF SHOPPING.

MAN: (SHOUTING) Oi, what's happened to my car?

INCREASINGLY ANNOYED, KENNY WALKS PAST THE CAR PARK ATTENDANT AND LADY, WHO ARE BOTH STILL IN A TRANCE, AND CALLS OVER TO THE MAN.

KENNY: (SHOUTING) Look into my eyes, look into my eyes . . .

WE SEE ANOTHER MAN WALKING THROUGH THE SHOT.

SECOND MAN: (SHOUTS) Me?

KENNY: (SHOUTS) No not you, him.

SEOND MAN: Oh, right.

THE FIRST MAN DROPS HIS SHOPPING BAGS AS KENNY BEGINS TO HYPNOTIZE HIM.

KENNY: (STILL SHOUTING, EXASPERATED) Look into my eyes, not around the eyes, don't look around the eyes, look into my eyes. (CLICKS) You're under. I never done it.

Look into my eyes, look into my eyes, the eyes, the eyes, not around the eyes, don't look around the eyes, look into my eyes you're under. You did not, repeat not, see me hit that car.

And to drink?

Um Bongo.

MAN IN RESTAURANT 3

INT: RESTAURANT. THE SAME MAN AS BEFORE IS SITTING AT HIS TABLE SURVEYING THE MENU AS THE WAITER WALKS OVER.

TOM V/O: Moanwheel in Throttle, a lunch order is being taken.

WAITER: Can I take your order, sir?

MAN: Yes, I'll have the wild truffle and Roquefort salad.

WAITER: Very good, sir.

MAN: And then the poached scallops with artichoke hearts.

WAITER: Will that be all?

MAN: Yes. And a bag of Monster Munch.

WAITER: And to drink?

MAN: Um Bongo.

MR MANN — BOOKSHOP

INT: BOOKSHOP. MR MANN ENTERS THE SHOP AND MAKES HIS WAY OVER TO THE COUNTER.

TOM V/O: It's nought o'clock and at this shop in Phlegm, Mr Mann is looking for a book. I read a book once, it was called Who on Earth is Tom Baker?

ROY: (IN AN UNNATURALLY STIFF VOICE) Hello, I did not know you liked books.

MR MANN: (JUST AS STIFFLY) Hello, yes, I like books very much.

ROY: Are you looking for anything in particular?

MR MANN: Not really, I was just wondering if you had any books on medieval English music between the dates 1356 and 1390?

ROY: Erm, I can't see anything here, Margaret knows all the books, one moment. (TURNS AND SHOUTS) Margaret? Margaret?

THERE IS A VERY LONG, UNCOMFORTABLE PAUSE.

MARGARET: (FROM UPSTAIRS) Yes?

ROY: (SHOUTING) There's a gentleman here wants to know if we've got any books on medieval English music dating between 1356 and 1390.

MARGARET: Paperback or hardback?

ROY: (TO MR MANN) Paperback or hardback?

MR MANN: Oh you know me, I'm easy.

PAUSE.

ROY: (SHOUTS) He says he's easy.

MR MANN: There should be one, over by the Mike Gatting autobiography.

ROY PICKS UP A NEARBY BOOK, AND SHOWS IT TO MR MANN.

ROY: Oh yes, here we are, '*The History of Medieval Music, 1356–1390*'.

ROY PASSES IT TO MR MANN, WHO HOLDS OUT HIS HAND BUT STARES BLANKLY AHEAD AS THE BOOK FALLS ON THE DESK.

MR MANN: Sorry, I didn't grip in time.

ROY TRIES ONCE MORE TO PASS THE BOOK TO MR MANN. THIS TIME IT BOUNCES OFF HIS OUTSTRETCHED, MOTIONLESS HAND.

MR MANN: Sorry, I gripped too soon that time, you may have to hold it.

ROY: Right, well, what do you reckon?

MR MANN: How many pages does it have?

ROY: Erm (CHECKS), three hundred and twelve.

MR MANN: Oh, I was hoping for something more along the three hundred and six mark

ROY: Right.

MR MANN: Do you think the author might be interested in rewriting his work to cut it down? Maybe if you cut out all the 'o's you might lose six pages there?

ROY: (CLEARLY BAFFLED) I, I don't think so, no.

MR MANN: Maybe I'm being too specific?

ROY: You are being a little specific, yes.

MR MANN: OK, have you got any books . . .

THERE FOLLOWS A VERY LONG PAUSE.

I was just wondering if you had any books on medieval English music between the dates 1356 and 1390?

Erm, I can't see anything here, Margaret knows all the books, one moment. Margaret? Margaret?

ROY: Have I got any books?

MR MANN: Yes.

ROY: (INDICATING THE SHOP'S SHELVES WITH A SWEEP OF THE HAND) Well, yes, we've got hundreds of them.

MR MANN: I'll take them, please.

CLEARLY PUZZLED, ROY LAUGHS TO HIMSELF, GETS A BOX OUT FROM UNDER THE COUNTER AND BEGINS TO FILL IT WITH BOOKS.

ROY: Oh right, oh. You must really like reading!

MR MANN: (DEADPAN, STARING STRAIGHT AHEAD) Oh, no. Unfortunately I'm blind.

ROY LOOKS SURPRISED AND SADDENED BY THIS NEWS. THEN, AFTER A PAUSE, HE CAN'T RESIST WAVING IN FRONT OF MR MANN'S FACE.

THERE IS A LONG PAUSE.

MR MANN WAVES BACK.

BUBBLES DEVERE – CHEQUE

EXT: HILL GRANGE HEALTH SPA. OUT ON THE LAWN, WE SEE A LARGE GROUP OF GUESTS RELAXING ON SUN
LOUNGERS, READING MAGAZINES.

TOM V/O: It's five to Pamela, and at this health spa in Chomp the guests are working
hard.

A FITNESS INSTRUCTOR STANDS IN FRONT OF THE GROUP OF RELAXING GUESTS. EACH HOLDING UP A MAGAZINE,
THE GUESTS FOLLOW THE INSTRUCTOR'S DIRECTIONS.

INSTRUCTOR: And turn the page . . . and rest.

INT: OFFICE. MR HUTTON, THE MANAGER OF THE HEALTH FARM, IS IN A MEETING WITH AN EMPLOYEE, SIMONE.

MR HUTTON: Possibly here at Hill Grange there is a need for some restructuring. Now, you
know that Jacqueline is leaving us.

SIMONE: Oh yes.

MR HUTTON: So from Monday . . . (THERE IS A KNOCK AT THE DOOR) Come in.

BUBBLES APPEARS IN THE DOORWAY AND STANDS THERE DRAMATICALLY, DRESSED ONLY IN A WHITE TOWEL.

BUBBLES: Hello, darling.

Hello, darling.

MR HUTTON: Oh, hello Mrs DeVere.

BUBBLES: Call me Bubbles, everybody does.

MR HUTTON: Mrs DeVere, I'm just in the middle of something.

BUBBLES: Simone, darling, would you be a darling and leave me and Mr Hutton alone for a moment? Thank you, darling. (AS SIMONE WALKS TOWARDS THE DOOR, BUBBLES ADDS IN A STAGE WHISPER) Not a word of this to anyone.

SIMONE LEAVES AND SHUTS THE DOOR.

BUBBLES: (SEDUCTIVELY) We're alone.

MR HUTTON: Have you got the cheque?

BUBBLES HOLDS UP A CHEQUE AND WAFTS IT, NONCHALANTLY.

BUBBLES: It's all here darling, all the treatments, all the food, bed and board for the last five months.

MR HUTTON: Great.

BUBBLES: Seventeen thousand, three hundred pounds, darling.

MR HUTTON: Thank you.

BUBBLES: (LOWERING HER VOICE, HER TONE CONSPIRATORIAL) But we don't need the cheque do we, darling.

MR HUTTON: Yes, we do.

BUBBLES: No, we don't.

BUBBLES RIPS UP THE CHEQUE, AND BEGINS TO HUM STRIPTEASE MUSIC AS SHE MAKES HER WAY TOWARDS MR HUTTON'S DESK, DROPPING HER TOWEL AND DANCING AS SHE GOES.

BUBBLES : Because . . . (SINGS) da da da . . . sorry . . . da da da da . . .

NOW COMPLETELY NAKED, BUBBLES ENDS THE STRIP
BY TOSSING HER WIG OFF AND, KNEELING ON A CHAIR,
BENDS OVER TO PRESENT MR HUTTON WITH AN
ENORMOUS BARE BACKSIDE.

BUBBLES: (OVER HER SHOULDER, SEDUCTIVELY) Be
quick, Mr Hutton, I have a colonic at
three.

LOU AND ANDY — TREE

EXT: PARK. WE SEE AN EMPTY WHEELCHAIR SITTING BY
A TREE.

TOM V/O: Lou Todd has bought two ice
creams, both for his friend Andy.

AS LOU MAKES HIS WAY BACK TO ANDY'S WHEELCHAIR,
HE REALIZES THAT IT IS EMPTY AND BREAKS INTO A
RUN, WORRIED.

LOU: Andy . . . Andy, where are you?

THE CAMERA PANS UP TO SHOW ANDY SITTING HIGH UP
IN THE BRANCHES OF THE TREE.

ANDY: Up here.

LOU: How did you get up there?

ANDY: I fell.

WE CUT TO A SCENE OF SEVERAL BURLY FIREMEN
LIFTING ANDY BACK INTO HIS WHEELCHAIR. LOU IS
CLEARLY HUGELY RELIEVED, AND STROLLS ALONG WITH
ONE OF THE FIREMAN, THANKING HIM.

LOU: Oh, thank you so much, thank you.
Oh, I was worried sick. What a kerfuffle.

IN THE BACKGROUND, WE SEE ANDY SITTING IN HIS
WHEELCHAIR. HE MIMES HOLDING AN OBJECT IN HIS
HANDS, CLEARLY REALIZES THAT HE HAS FORGOTTEN
SOMETHING, AND JUMPS OUT OF THE CHAIR. WHILE LOU

How did
you get
up
there?

I fell.

AND THE FIREMAN SPEAK, ANDY RACES UP THE FIREMEN'S LADDER, WHICH IS STILL AGAINST THE TREE, RECOVERS A FOOTBALL FROM A HIGH BRANCH, AND SLIDES DOWN THE LADDER ATHLETICALLY.

FIREMAN: How did he get up there?

LOU: Well I've absolutely no idea. As you can see, he's not the most able bodied person there is. He's confined to a wheelchair and I push that, so I'm not even sure he's got the strength in his arms to get up a tree, I mean it's a mystery, I mean something for Arthur C Clarke to put in *The Arthur C Clarke's Mysterious World* or Toyah Wilcox would sing about in her song 'It's a Mystery' and I think the best thing I can do now is get him home, early bath, early to bed and they say a good idea is a nice hot warm milky drink like a cup of cocoa or something. (TURNING, TO FIND ANDY CALMLY SITTING IN HIS WHEELCHAIR WITH THE FOOTBALL) OK, we'd better get you home, young man.

ANDY: Yeah, I know.

LOU STARTS TO WHEEL ANDY OFF, PAST THE FIREMEN.

LOU: Thank you. Oh, did they bring the ball down as well?

ANDY: Yeah.

LOU: That was kind of them.

TOM V/O: And so our visit to Little Britain has come to an end. I must go now, because a man has come into the room and he's trying to pull my clothes off. I must just find out what he wants. Good tie.

AS LOU WALKS OFF WHEELING THE HAIR ALONG, ANDY CHUCKS THE FOOTBALL AWAY.

ANDY: Where's my Funny Foot?

I mean it's a **mystery**, I mean something for Arthur C Clarke to put in *The Arthur C Clarke's Mysterious World* or Toyah Wilcox would sing about in her song 'It's a **Mystery**'

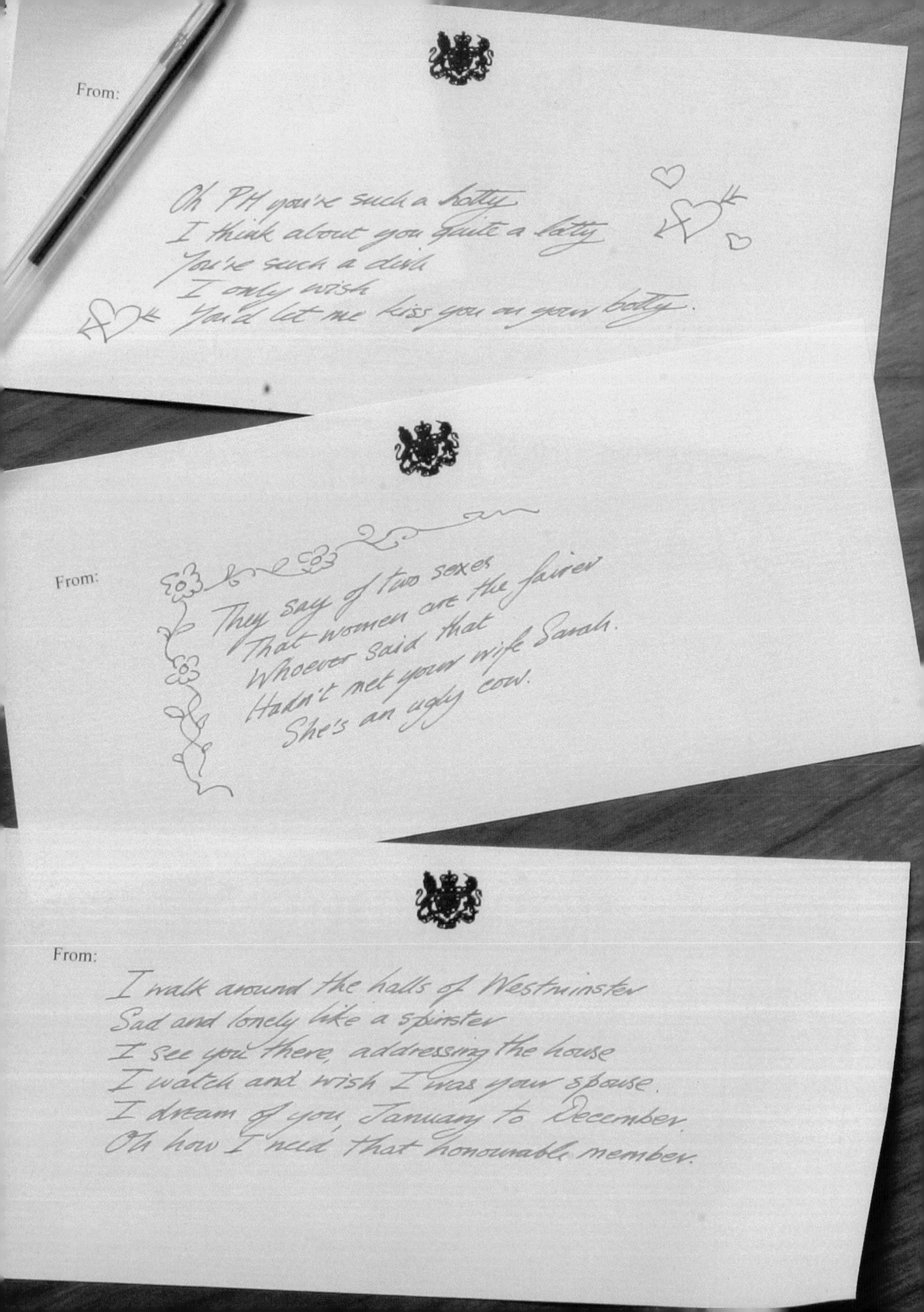

Oh PH you're such a hotty
I think about you quite a lotty
You're such a dish
I only wish
You'd let me kiss you on your botty.

They say of two sexes
That women are the fairer
Whoever said that
Hadn't met your wife Sarah.
She's an ugly cow.

I walk around the halls of Westminster
Sad and lonely like a spinster
I see you there, addressing the house
I watch and wish I was your spouse.
I dream of you, January to December.
Oh how I need that honourable member.

From:

Tall and lean, your name is Michael,
I'd like to ride you like a cycle.
You caught my eye at the party conference
All I could think about was your
generous circumference.

- Mich...

From:

You live at Ten Downing Street.
Strong, powerful, with nice big feet
Which mother always told me was a
good indication of penis size.

om:

Let's run away, P.M. Just you and me
And find a cottage by the sea
Lovely and clean, unspoilt, no litter.
And you can take me up the shops,
And then we can come home and have sex.

EPISODE

TOM V/O: Britain, Britain, Britain. Why would you ever want to leave? Anybody who goes on holiday abroad is a traitor. I bloody love it here, bloody love it. We produce the best films, the finest cuisine, and our dogs are relatively Rabies-free, and this is all thanks to the peoples of Britain. Let us look at them in this programme, in which we now look at them now. Boom boom, shake the room.

LOU AND ANDY — BOWLING

EXT: A BUSY BOWLING ALLEY.

TOM V/O: Ten pin bowling is a very difficult sport, but it is easier than eleven pin bowling.

WITH LOU CHEERING HIM ON, ANDY BENDS DOWN FROM HIS WHEELCHAIR AND DROPS A BOWLING BALL STRAIGHT INTO THE GUTTER. WE THEN WATCH THE BALL ROLL, PAINFULLY SLOWLY, THE FULL LENGTH OF THE GUTTER . . .

LOU: One, two, three. Yes, yes, yes, yes, yes, yes, yes, yes, yes, yes, yes, yes, yes, yes, yes, yes, yes, yes, yes, yes, yes, yes, yes, yes, yes, yes, yes, yes, yes. Oh ho ho! Unlucky. Right, you've got one more go, and maybe that ball was a bit heavy, you want a different one?

ANDY POINTS VAGUELY BEHIND HIMSELF WITHOUT LOOKING.

ANDY: Yeah, I want that one.

LOU: Ok, there you go. (LOU'S MOBILE RINGS) Oh, excuse me.

AS LOU ANSWERS THE CALL, DISTRACTED, ANDY JUMPS OUT OF HIS WHEELCHAIR AND RUNS DOWN THE ALLEY HOLDING THE BOWLING BALL. GOING RIGHT UP TO THE PINS, HE KNOCKS THEM ALL DOWN AND RUNS BACK, CELEBRATING.

LOU: Hello? Lou Todd? Oh hello there Chris, how are you? Yes, I've taken him bowling. A bit of a kerfuffle, but he seems to be enjoying it. No, I'm winning, it's 75-3. I'll get him to call you back later. Ta ra. (TURNING ROUND TO LOOK DOWN THE ALLEY) Oh. You've got a strike!

ANDY: Yeah, I know.

LOU: I didn't even have to help you, well done.

VICKY POLLARD – BLAZIN' SQUAD

EXT: THE STAGE DOOR OF A THEATRE. A CROWD OF GIRLS IS QUEUING TO GET BACKSTAGE.

TOM V/O: Backstage at the Blazin' Squad concert, fans are clammering to meet the band. I myself loathe groups like Blazin Squad, I much prefer So Solid.

VICKY APPEARS AND STARTS TO PUSH HER WAY THROUGH THE CROWD, TOWARDS THE BOUNCER.

VICKY: Get out the way get out the way get out the way *GET OUT OF THE WAY!* get out the way get out the way get out of the way. (TO THE DOORMAN) I'm here with Blazin' Squad.

DOORMAN: Can we see your passes, please?

VICKY: No but yeah but no but yeah but no but because what happened was is that I did have passes but Kelly Appleby snatched them all and burned them because Ruth Harman who's bitch number one told her that I nicked one of her dayglo hair scrunchies but I never. Anyway don't listen to her because everyone knows her fanny goes sideways.

A GIRL IN THE CROWD HELPFULLY MAKES A FACE BY PUTTING HER FINGERS IN HER MOUTH AND PULLING HER LIPS WIDE APART.

GIRL IN CROWD: Yeah I've seen it, it's like this.

DOORMAN: No one's coming in without a pass.

A ROUGH-LOOKING GIRL PUSHES THROUGH AND CHALLENGES VICKY.

GIRL IN CROWD: Excuse me, mingers to the back of the queue.

VICKY: Shut up! No but yeah but no because I am definitely on the list.

DOORMAN: What's your name, then?

VICKY TRIES TO SNEAK A LOOK AT THE GUEST LIST.

VICKY: (SHEEPISHLY) Er, 'Sony Records' . . .

DOORMAN: I don't think so.

VICKY: Oh my God I so can't believe you just said that. I so *am* on the list because this guy from Sony records took me dancing to Mis-Teeq who I completely hate in the audience on *CD:UK* and I met Cat Deeley and she's got a really hairy face. But anyway this guy from Sony records said he really wants to like sign me up and like turn me into the next Beyoncé. And it was good but then I forgot because we was all round the back of Argos watching Carrie Stevens getting bummed by the bloke who works in Cash Converters.

GIRL IN CROWD: You ain't on the list.

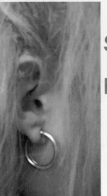

Shutup!Nobutyeahbutno
becauseIamdefinitelyonthelist.

VICKY: Shut up, (TO BOUNCER) I am so am.

DOORMAN: I ain't letting you in.

VICKY: No but yeah but no because if you don't let me in Blazin' Squad are well gonna give you beatings because I've actually met them already anyway actually down at the Radio One roadshow in Weston Super Mare. You remember it was the time I got fingered by Chris Moyles and Hayley Everett said she reckoned she saw Jo Whiley taking a dump

EPISODE TWO

in the sea. But anyway I have met Blazin' Squad and they said I should definitely come back stage and see them and do them. And anyway I do know them because I'm their sister and if Roman Gordon says I'm not don't listen to him because everyone knows he's mental because he once shoved his knob through Miss Maynard's letter box.

GIRL IN CROWD: Such a liar.

VICKY: (GROWLING) Shut up.

DOORMAN: I won't tell you again. You're not – coming – in. (HE KISSES HIS TEETH MENACINGLY)

VICKY LOOKS RESIGNED AND IN A COOL, BUSINESSLIKE WAY, UNZIPS HER JACKET AND PUFFS HER CHEST OUT.

VICKY: Alright, lads. One at a time.

EMILY AND FLORENCE – TENNIS

EXT: GRASS TENNIS COURTS ON A SUMMER'S DAY.

TOM V/O: The game of tennis was invented in 1982 by Dr Jonathan Tennis, when he had the idea of fusing the popular sports of badminton and Swingball.

TWO MEN IN TENNIS GEAR MAKE THEIR WAY ONTO THE COURTS.

TENNIS PLAYER 1: It's mixed doubles today, innit?

TENNIS PLAYER 2: Yeah.

TENNIS PLAYER 1: Those two we played last time were gorgeous.

TENNIS PLAYER 2: Yeah, I hope these two are fit.

TENNIS PLAYER 1: Did you get their names?

TENNIS PLAYER 2: Yeah, they're up on the board – Emily and Florence.

EMILY AND FLORENCE STROLL ONTO THE COURT IN OLD-FASHIONED, FLOOR-LENGTH TENNIS DRESSES, GIRLISHLY EXCITED.

EMILY: Anyone for tennis?

FLORENCE: Good afternoon, we're here for the mixed doubles.

TENNIS PLAYER 1: (CONFUSED) We're expecting two ladies . . .

FLORENCE: Oh, sorry.

FLORENCE BEGINS TO TURN AND WALK AWAY, BUT EMILY STOPS HER.

EMILY: (LAUGHING TO COVER THE EMBARRASSMENT) No, no, no, that is us, two ladies.

Well, have you got any balls?

TENNIS PLAYER 2: (UNCONVINCED) Right . . .

EMILY WHISPERS TO FLORENCE.

EMILY: Florence, do as I do and watch how they don't suspect a thing. (CALLING OUT) Ready, gentlemen!

TENNIS PLAYER 2: Well, have you got any balls?

EMILY: Oh no, we are ladies.

TENNIS PLAYER 2: Tennis balls . . .

EMILY: Oh, sorry, silly me, I thought you meant bollocks. (FLIRTILY, LEADING HIM ONTO THE COURT) You're with me.

FLORENCE IS LEFT WITH THE OTHER TENNIS PLAYER. THERE IS AN AWKWARD, BLOKISH SILENCE.

FLORENCE: (IN A DEEP, MAN'S VOICE) Alright?

WE CUT TO THE GAME ITSELF. EMILY TOSSES THE BALL UP AS IF TO SERVE, AND THEN ALLOWS IT TO DROP PATHETICALLY TO THE FLOOR.

EMILY: Ready! Oh, oh, oh, being a lady I'm quite exhausted, aren't you, Florence?

FLORENCE: Oh yes, absolutely knackered, time for barley water, I think.

EMILY: Oh yes please, Florence my dear.

EMILY AND FLORENCE WALK OFF THE COURT AND SIT AT A TABLE POURING DRINKS. THE TENNIS PLAYERS WATCH THEM GO, PUZZLED, BEFORE FOLLOWING THEM.

EMILY: Are you enjoying the game, Florence my dear?

FLORENCE: Oh yes Emily, it's positively nail-biting, isn't it? Chin chin!

TENNIS PLAYER 2: Are you guys going to be long?

EMILY: Oh we'll be right with you, we're just going to have some scones.

INT: SHOWER ROOM. THE TWO TENNIS PLAYERS STRIP OFF AND MAKE THEIR WAY INTO THE COMMUNAL SHOWERS.

TENNIS PLAYER 2: I've had better games.

TENNIS PLAYER 1: Yeah. And those two have to be the strangest looking women I've ever seen.

EMILY AND FLORENCE SUDDENLY APPEAR, NAKED, ALONGSIDE THEM IN THE SHOWERS.

EMILY: (SCANDALIZED) Do you mind?

PSYCHIATRIST'S OFFICE 1

INT: PSYCHIATRIST'S OFFICE. A PSYCHIATRIST IS LISTENING TO HIS PATIENT.

TOM V/O: It is almost Terry o'clock, and at this psychiatrist's office, the session is coming to an end.

FEMALE PATIENT: . . . felt alone, and that's when we started having a sexual relationship.

PSYCHIATRIST: (GENTLY) And this was with Colin, your brother-in-law?

FEMALE PATIENT: Yes.

PSYCHIATRIST: And what did you feel?

FEMALE PATIENT: Um, guilt.

PSYCHIATRIST: Shame?

FEMALE PATIENT: Yes.

THE PSYCHIATRIST LOOKS AT HIS WATCH.

PSYCHIATRIST: (WITH FEELING, SOFTLY) Ok, we're going to have to leave it there, but we'll talk more next week.

FEMALE PATIENT: Thank you.

THE PATIENT GETS UP FROM THE COUCH AND LEAVES THE ROOM.

AS SOON AS THE DOOR CLOSES, THE PSYCHIATRIST LEAPS TO HIS PHONE AND DIALS A NUMBER.

PSYCHIATRIST: Hello? It's me. You'll never guess what – she's only having it off with his brother! Yeah I know, cheeky cow!

MARJORIE DAWES/FATFIGHTERS — PAT

INT: A FATFIGHTERS MEETING. PAT IS STANDING ON THE SCALES, WHILE MARJORIE READS THE DISPLAY.

TOM V/O: If a policeman stops a fat person and discovers they are carrying chocolate, he is permitted to shoot them. Hence diet classes, like this one, are very popular.

MARJORIE: Right, well, this week, Pat has lost four pounds. (THE OTHER FATFIGHTERS APPLAUD AS PAT RETURNS TO HER SEAT) Pigs *can* fly.

PAT: See, I told you I'd lose a stone by Christmas.

MARJORIE: Yeah, next Christmas maybe.

PAUL: (TO PAT) You won't have to come here for much longer.

PAT: Yeah, that will be nice. Won't have to put up with Marjorie any more!

MARJORIE: We'll see. Ok, before we go any further, I've got to tell you FatFighters has brought out a brand-new range of delicious new low-calories puddings. They are new and they are called Fatty Treats. You've seen the adverts? Yeah? (SINGS) 'Fatty Treats, treats for the fatty, boink'. Oh well anyway, what I've got is I've got normal éclairs, and I've got new, they are new, brand-new, low-calories FatFighters Fatty Treats éclairs, and I want to see if we can tell the difference. So can we have please a volunteer? (SEEING A HAND GO UP) Sorry Meera, I was really just thinking of the English people. Erm, Pat, come and join me.

PAT: (NOT KEEN) It's alright, Marjorie.

MARJORIE: No, come on, you're the star slimmer. (PAT WALKS OVER TO MARJORIE AND SITS DOWN) Wobble wobble wobble . . . Right, what we'll do is I'm going to put this blind fold on you. Right? No peeping.

PAT: Oh, it's quite tight, Marjorie

MARJORIE: (THROUGH HER TEETH) Well it's got to be tight, because I know you fat people are very devious, now you are lying, Pat, and I do mean that nicely. Right, now I've got two éclairs here, and I want you to see if you can guess which is the low-calorie one. Alright? Ready?

PAT: I'm not really eating puddings at the moment.

MARJORIE: Here we go.

MARJORIE POPS THE END OF AN ÉCLAIR INTO PAT'S MOUTH.

PAT: Ooh, mmm, that is nice, though. Very creamy.

MARJORIE: Ok, now try this one. Yes? Now, can you taste the difference?

PAT: No.

MARJORIE: No, you can't. Well let me tell you that the second éclair you had was the low-calorie one.

WHILE PAT SITS BLINDFOLDED MARJORIE KEEPS TALKING, ALL THE WHILE SHOVING WHOLE ÉCLAIRS INTO PAT'S MOUTH.

MARJORIE: Hey? Why don't you have another, hmm? Go on. There you go. Why don't you have a second one, go on, get them in your fat gob. Well why not, they're low calorie, she's not going to put on an ounce. Oh no, hang on a minute Pat, I've just made a dreadful mistake, those are the full-fat ones. 400 calories per éclair, oh my God . . . She's going to explode, quick, spit it out, all of it quickly, all of it, quickly, all of it, quickly, all of it, quickly, all of it, quickly, all of it, quickly, all of it.

> oh my God . . . She's going to explode, quick, spit it out, all of it quickly, all of it, quickly, all of it, quickly, all of it, quickly, all of it, quickly, all of it, quickly, all of it.

AFTER SHE HAS SPAT A BIT OF ÉCLAIR ONTO A PLATE, PAT LOOKS VERY DISAPPOINTED.

MARJORIE: Shame on you, Pat, shame on you. You've let everyone down. Right, well, better put a couple of them pounds back on, hadn't we? And we'll see you next week. Oh hang on a minute Pat, you've just got a little bit of cream in your hair, wait there. (MARJORIE CUTS OFF A HUGE CLUMP OF PAT'S HAIR WITH A PAIR OF SCISSORS) There you go. Ok, lovely. Now, I want to talk to you all about dust . . .

WORKMEN

EXT: A GRAND-LOOKING MANOR HOUSE. TWO WORKMEN ARE SITTING ON THE PATIO TAKING A BREAK. AN OLDER WOMAN, MRS B, APPEARS FROM THE HOUSE'S FRONT DOOR, ACCOMPANIED BY SEVERAL DOGS.

TOM V/O: There are hundreds of dogs in Britain. The biggest, the Blue Setter, is as tall as the Houses of Parliament. The smallest, the Boodle, is invisible to the naked eye.

MRS B MAKES HER WAY OVER TO THE BUILDERS.

MRS B: Hello, men.

WORKMEN: Hello, Mrs B, we're just having a cuppa.

MRS B: Yes I saw, I thought I'd bring you up some biscuits.

WORKMEN: Oh, thanks very much, Mrs B.

SPEAKING TO THE WORKMEN VERY MUCH AS IF THEY WERE DOGS, THE WOMAN STANDS BEHIND THEM AND BEGINS TO THROW BISCUITS OUT INTO THE GARDEN. ONE OF THE WORKMEN GETS UP TO RETRIEVE THEM, WHILE THE OTHER STAYS SEATED AND BEGS, RATHER RELUCTANTLY, FOR A BISCUIT OF HIS OWN.

MRS B: There you go. Fetch, fetch. There's a good boy. Fetch. Good boy, good boy, good boy, good boy. There's one, there's one, where's the other one? Where's the other one? *Good boy*, who's a good boy? One for you, beg, beg, there's a good boy, there's a good boy!

SHE PRAISES HIM BY RUBBING HIS HEAD AS HE EATS HIS BISCUIT.

VIV — ID PARADE

EXT: THE ENTRANCE TO A POLICE STATION. WE SEE VIV WALKING IN AND STOPPING TO STARE LUSTFULLY AND SAY 'PHWOAR' AT THE SIGHT OF A PASSING POLICEMAN.

TOM V/O: It is a quarter to Gran and Grandpa Moses, and woman Viv Tudor has been requested to attend an identity parade.

POLICE OFFICER: Ok, now take your time, alright?

VIV: Yeah. Yeah.

POLICE OFFICER: And let me know if you recognize anyone at all.

THE POLICEMAN LEADS VIV ALONG THE LINE OF POTENTIAL CRIMINALS.

VIV: (COMPOSING HERSELF) Recognize anyone at all, yeah, yeah. (PASSING THE FIRST MAN, SPEAKING SOFTLY) No. I don't know . . . (PASSING THE SECOND MAN) No. No. No. (PASSING THE THIRD MAN) Oh he's *gorgeous*, oh what a hunk! Look at that scar, ooh, there's a wrong-un and no mistakes! Phwoar!

POLICE OFFICER: Do you recognize him?

VIV: No, no.

VIV: (FILING PAST THE FOURTH MAN) No. (MAN NUMBER FIVE) Oh he's *gorgeous*, oh what a dream boat! Puts me in mind of a young Omar Shariff, oh he can rob my bank any day! Phwoar!

POLICE OFFICER: (SOFTLY BUT INSISTENTLY) But was he involved in the robbery?

VIV: No, no, shame but no.

THEY PASS THE SIXTH MAN.

VIV: Oh he's *gorgeous*, phwoar, he can point his weapon at me any time he likes. Phwoar!

POLICE OFFICER: (LOSING PATIENCE) But was he *there*?

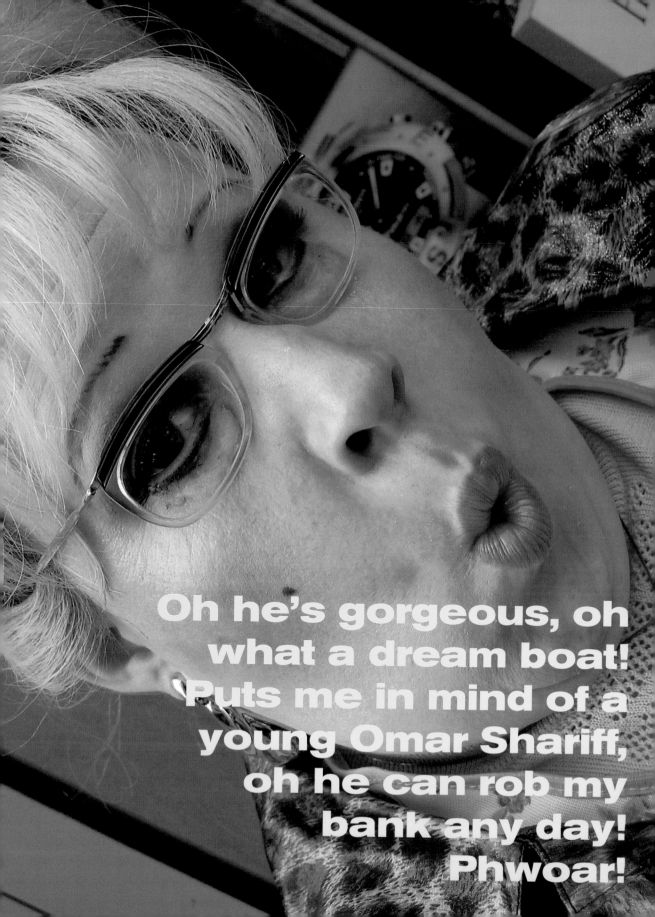

'Cause he's **gorgeous!** Oh, proper gorge...

VIV: Oh yeah, he was the one with the gun.

POLICE OFFICER: Great, thanks.

VIV: But you're not going to arrest him are you?

POLICE OFFICER: Yes.

VIV: But you can't, you mustn't. Anyway, you'll never get a conviction.

POLICE OFFICER: Why not?

VIV: 'Cause he's *gorgeous*! Oh, proper gorge...

SEBASTIAN AND MICHAEL — TV INTERVIEW

INT: A BUSY TV STUDIO.

TOM V/O: The Prime Minister is preparing for an important television interview. I never watch television myself, apart from Emmerdale, Corrie and Eastenders. Oh, and Hollyoaks.

THE PROGRAMME'S PRESENTER, GAVIN ESLER, IS BEING GIVEN A FEW FINAL TOUCHES BY THE MAKE-UP ARTIST WHILE THE PRIME MINISTER, SEATED BESIDE HIM, GETS READY FOR THE INTERVIEW.

FLOOR MANAGER: Now we're in studio 20. Seconds . . .

SEBASTIAN WAFTS GAVIN'S MAKE-UP WOMAN AWAY, BUZZING.

SEBASTIAN: Pss pss pss pss pss pss buzz buzz buzz. (TO GAVIN) So, erm, what you going to ask him?

GAVIN: I wouldn't want to spoil the surprise now, would I?

SEBASTIAN: (TRYING TO GRAB HIS SCRIPT) Let me have a look.

GAVIN: No.

MICHAEL: I'm sure I can handle Gavin by myself, thank you.

O/S: Ten seconds

SEBASTIAN: (TO GAVIN) Ok, but promise me you won't mention anything about the man who runs the airlines giving money to the party?

MICHAEL: Get off the set!

GAVIN: (TO THE CAMERA) Good evening. The airline scandal that has engulfed the government now threatens to topple the Prime Minister.

OFF SET, SEBASTIAN BEGINS TO HECKLE GAVIN.

SEBASTIAN: Oh, you bitch.

GAVIN: He's here with me live in the studio. Prime Minister, welcome

MICHAEL: Good evening.

GAVIN: Prime Minister, can you explain to me how on Wednesday, we hear that the government has granted exclusive transatlantic routes to Embassy airlines, and then yesterday it emerges that the chairman of Embassy, Sir Brian Dean, has previously donated over a million pounds to your party?

SEBASTIAN: (CHEERLEADING) Come on, Michael!

MICHAEL: (SMOOTHLY) The two events are completely unrelated. Sir Brian gave that money as a private individual.

SEBASTIAN: (DANCING, OFF SET) Go Michael, go Michael, go Michael, go Michael.

GAVIN: Prime Minister, I do think that there are a lot of unanswered questions . . .

MICHAEL: Go ahead.

SEBASTIAN: (CATCALLING) Yeah, go ahead, dear.

FLOOR MANAGER: Shhh.

SEBASTIAN: Shhh!

GAVIN: Would Embassy airlines have been granted exclusive use of those routes if that donation had not been made?

SEBASTIAN: (CALLS) Oh, give it a rest!

MICHAEL: I've already answered this question in the House.

GAVIN: (TO CAMERA) In fact, we can see that footage right now.

SEBASTIAN: Oh, here we go.

FLOOR MANAGER: VT for one minute.

GAVIN: Would someone please get that man out of the studio?

SEBASTIAN: Well don't worry, I'm going, and I tell you what guv, only came here tonight because I thought I was going to meet Paxman, he's much better looking than you.

SEBASTIAN LEAVES IN A HUFF. GAVIN TURNS TO THE PRIME MINISTER, LOOKING CONCERNED.

GAVIN: Paxman's not better looking than me, is he?

MICHAEL: (MEANINGFULLY) No, you're lovely.

PSYCHIATRIST'S OFFICE 2

INT: PSYCHIATRIST'S OFFICE.

MALE PATIENT: (ANGUISHED) . . . and that was about the same time I started seeing prostitutes.

PSYCHIATRIST: Do you think that paying for sex has become an addiction?

MALE PATIENT: Yes. I do feel it's out of my control now.

PSYCHIATRIST: It's become a compulsion?

MALE PATIENT: Definitely.

THE PSYCHIATRIST CHECKS HIS WATCH.

PSYCHIATRIST: (GENTLY) Ok, well we've actually gone over a little but, er, we'll pick up on this next time.

MALE PATIENT: Ok. Thanks.

THE PATIENT GETS UP, WALKS TO THE DOOR AND LEAVES.

AS SOON AS THE DOOR CLOSES, THE PSYCHIATRIST RACES TO THE PHONE AND DIALS.

PSYCHIATRIST: You were right, prossies! Well, you have to laugh, don't you? I know, dirty bastard.

KENNY CRAIG — GIRLFRIEND

EXT: STREET. A BIG, LUXURIOUS CAR PULLS UP OUTSIDE AN ORDINARY SUBURBAN HOUSE. THE CHAUFFEUR GETS OUT OF THE CAR AND WALKS ROUND TO OPEN ONE OF THE PASSENGER DOORS. A PAPERBOY STEPS OUT AND DELIVERS A NEWSPAPER TO THE HOUSE.

TOM V/O: It's early morning and in the outskirts of Slaughter, stage hypnotist Kenny Craig has spent the night with his girlfriend.

INT: A BEDROOM. KENNY IS SITTING ON THE BED, DRESSED, CONCENTRATING HARD ON TYING HIS SHOELACES.

KENNY: (MUTTERING TO HIMSELF) You can do this – left over right and . . . under.

KENNY'S GIRLFRIEND IS IN A TOWEL, IN THE PROCESS OF GETTING UP.

KENNY'S GIRLFRIEND: Are you not staying for breakfast?

KENNY: Er, I would but, er, mother's bought some croissants so, er, should probably be heading back.

KENNY'S GIRLFRIEND: You did enjoy last night, didn't you?

KENNY: Yes I did, I thought the love making was absolutely top notch.

KENNY'S GIRLFRIEND: (PUZZLED) It's funny, I can't remember that part.

STILL SITTING ON THE BED, KENNY LOOKS A LITTLE SHEEPISH.

KENNY'S GIRLFRIEND: (GOING OVER TO HER CHEST OF DRAWERS) I can't find any underwear, it keeps on going missing, you haven't seen any of it, have you?

LOOKING EVEN MORE SHEEPISH,, KENNY DECIDES TO GET UP AND HYPNOTIZE HER.

KENNY: Look into my eyes, look into my eyes, the eyes, the eyes, not around the eyes, don't look around my eyes, look into my eyes, (CLICKS HIS FINGERS) you're under. I have not been taking your underwear home, putting it on in my bedroom and then parading up and down in front of the mirror going, (RUNNING HIS HANDS OVER HIS CHEST AND BACKSIDE) 'Oh, oh, oh, oh'. Three – two – one . . . (CLICK) You're back in the room.

KENNY'S GIRLFRIEND COMES TO AND STARTS TO LOOK IN HER WARDROBE FOR SOMETHING TO WEAR.

KENNY'S GIRLFRIEND: And do you know, I can't find that red dress, you know, the silk one with the embroidery. The one I wore when we went to see 'We Will Rock You'.

LOOKING WORRIED, KENNY DECIDES TO HYPNOTIZE HER AGAIN.

KENNY: Look into my eyes, look into my eyes, the eyes, the eyes, not around the eyes, don't look around the eyes, look into my eyes, (CLICKS) you're under. I did not steal your red dress and then take it home and then wear it while doing the hoovering. Three – two – one, you're back in the room.

KENNY'S GIRLFRIEND: And you know, I can't find those stilettos, you know, those ones from Shelley's?

KENNY: (IMPATIENTLY) Look, I bought you those, I kind of think if I want to wear them I'll wear them.

THERE IS AN AWKWARD SILENCE. KENNY REALISES WHAT HE HAS SAID.

Look into my eyes, look into my eyes, the eyes, the eyes, not around the eyes, don't look around my eyes, look into my eyes, you're under. I have not been taking your underwear home, putting it on in my bedroom and then parading up and down in front of the mirror going, 'Oh, oh, oh, oh'.

MAN IN RESTAURANT 4

INT: RESTAURANT. WE SEE THE USUAL WAITER WALKING OVER TO SERVE THE SAME GENTLEMAN AS BEFORE.

WAITER: Can I take your order, sir?

MAN: Yes, I'll have the beef carpaccio to start. And then the braised lamb shank.

WAITER: Any vegetables?

MAN: Du jour.

WAITER: Very good, sir.

(PAUSE)

MAN: (CALLING AFTER HIM) And a Yorkie. Buttered.

And a Yorkie.
Buttered.

REHAB

INT: COMMUNITY CENTRE. A LARGE CIRCLE OF PEOPLE ARE SITTING IN A CIRCLE, WHILE SCOTTISH REHAB OFFICER DOUG STRIDES AROUND THE ROOM ENERGETICALLY.

TOM V/O: This is a drug rehab centre in Glasgee. I tried heroin once, but it didn't have any effect. Mind you, I was high on coke at the time.

DOUG: (ANIMATED) Ok, twenty words for heroin, go.

O/S: H.

DOUG: Good.

O/S: Brown

DOUG: Good.

O/S: Smack.

DOUG: Good.

O/S: Dragon.

DOUG: Good.

O/S: Skag.

DOUG: (ENGAGING) Good. Ok, so that's twenty. So why are you here? (SHOUTS ANGRILY) Because you're junkies, you're addicts, you're scum! Go on get out, all of you, get out of my sight! (EVERYBODY BEGINS TO GET UP, UNCERTAINLY) Stay where you are! (CALMLY) This is the road back.

OLD LADY: Excuse me . . .

DOUG: Yeah exactly, who am I to be telling youse about getting off the drugs? Well I've been there, ok? I've done it, I've read the book, I've seen the film, I've bought the T-shirt and got sick all down it – because I was on drugs. I know what it's like to have woken up so late because of drugs that I've missed *LK Today*, *Trisha* and most of *This Morning*.

This is a drug rehab centre in Glasgee. I tried heroin once, but it didn't have any effect. Mind you, I was high on coke at the time.

OLD LADY: I'm sorry about this, but I think I'm in the wrong room. I'm actually looking for the cake decorating class.

DOUG: (ADDRESSING THE CLASS) You know what this is, team? This is the very worst kind of junkie. 'I'm actually looking for the cake decorating class?' Well, maybe you are. (SOFTLY, INTO HER EAR) Hundreds and thousands, desiccated coconut and a wee sprinkling of (SHOUTS) *cocaine*! No more lies, no more excuses, you're an addict, you're scum! You're Laurel and

You know what this is, team? This is the very worst kind of junkie. 'I'm actually looking for the cake decorating class?' Well, maybe you are. Hundreds and thousands, desiccated coconut and a wee sprinkling of COCAINE!

Hardy the cartoon, you're soda-stream cola, you're *Grease 2*. Ok, go to your so-called cake decorating class. Get out that door and don't come back! (SHE BEGINS TO GET UP; HE ONCE AGAIN SOFTENS HIS TONE) Stay where you are, we'll help you. The most important word youse all need to learn is 'no'. (TURNING TO A YOUNG MAN) Spud, will you come and do a roleplay with me? (GENTLY, REASSURINGLY) Spud, Spuddy, you alright with this?

SPUD: Yeah.

DOUG: Yeah? Ok, so I'm the junkie, you're the dealer. Ask me if I want to buy any of the drugs.

SPUD: Do you want to buy any drugs?

DOUG: No. (TURNS BACK TO THE GROUP) And it's as simple as that. I really appreciate you doing that for me. Eh? Eh, Big Man?

HE GIVES SPUD A HUG.

OLD LADY: I don't want to be rude, but I really *am* here just for the cake decoration.

SPUD: Oh, it's just down the corridor

MAN IN CLINIC: Yeah, next room along.

OLD LADY: Oh, thank you.

DOUG: (GENTLY, APPARENTLY CONTRITE) Well of course, they do cake decoration here on a Monday, don't they? Sorry, it used to be Wednesdays. Yeah, let me help you with your bag.

OLD LADY: Oh, thank you.

DOUG: (APOLOGETICALLY) Yeah, sorry, what do you want to be sat here with all these junkies for? (BEGINS SHOUTING) Do you think I'm stupid?! Get back to your seat, you're a junkie! You're a loser, you're a leech! You're 'Carrot Confidential', you're Kellogg's Banana Bubbles, you're Stephen Gateley's solo career, you're Carol Thatcher! Siddown! (SOFTLY) You're going to be fine. (ANIMATED) Ok, fifty words for cocaine, go!

OLD LADY: Coke?

DOUG: Ok, that's fifty.

DR LAWRENCE AND ANNE – SKETCHING

EXT: A LARGE GARDEN. ANNE SITS ON A BENCH BY THE FLOWER BEDS, APPARENTLY MAKING SKETCHES IN A BOOK. WE SEE THE TWO DOCTORS STROLLING TOWARDS HER WHILE SHE SQUAWKS TO HERSELF AND CONCENTRATES ON HER DRAWINGS.

TOM V/O: At this park in Bent, Dr Lawrence has brought Dr Beagrie along to observe one of his patients.

ANNE: (SKETCHING) Eh, eh ,eh!

DR LAWRENCE: I don't know if you know, but our Anne is a very keen artist.

ANNE: Eh, eh ,eh!

DR LAWRENCE: Hm, she's actually getting better all the time. She particularly likes to draw the trees and the flowers.

ANNE: (CONCENTRATING ON A FIDDLY BIT) Eh, eh, eh!

ANNE GETS UP AND WALKS AWAY FROM THE BENCH, LEAVING HER SKETCH BOOK BEHIND.

ANNE: (HAPPILY) Eh, eh, eh!

LET ME EH-EH-EH-EH-EH YOU!

Robbie finds love with Anne

Ex-Take That star Robbie Williams was sensationally snapped last night for the first time with his new love Anne.

They were having dinner at London's fashionable Angus Steakhouse restaurant. An onlooker said, 'There was lots of holding hands and kissing. The pair couldn't keep their hands off each other. They looked very much in love.' According to reports, ex-Boyzone star Robbie enjoyed steak and chips while Anne also had steak and chips.

Could It Be Magic

A friend of the ex-Bad Boys Inc star said, 'It's early days but

Robbie is very keen on Anne. He thinks she's really sexy and can't get enough of her slippers and cardigan. The only problem for the pair is their conflicting schedules, with Robbie hard at work recording his latest album and preparing for a world tour and Anne busy going "Eh eh eh!" a lot.'

Never Forget

Ex-Upside Down star Robbie has previously been linked to a string of beauties including Geri

Halliwell, Rachel Hunter and that one out of All Saints who's now with that bloke out of Oasis. Meanwhile Anne is also no stranger to the limelight, having been spotted on dates with Blue's Antony Costa, shamed children's TV presenter Jamie Theakston and ex-Dr Who star Sylvester McCoy.

A Million Love Songs

A spokesman for Robbie refused to comment last night over rumours that the red-hot couple were thinking of getting engaged. Anne, too, was keeping tight-lipped, saying only 'Eh eh eh!'.

DR LAWRENCE: Ooh, she's left her sketch book behind.

THE TWO DOCTORS WALK OVER TO THE BENCH. THEY PICK UP THE BOOK AND BEGIN TO LEAF THROUGH ANNE'S WORK. WE SEE THAT IN FACT, SHE HAS BEEN MAKING A FLICK-BOOK OF A LARGE PENIS BECOMING ERECT AND EJACULATING.

DR LAWRENCE: She makes me very proud.

DENNIS WATERMAN — SIR ANDREW LLOYD WEBBER

INT: JEREMY'S OFFICE. JEREMY IS STANDING AT THE DESK WITH SIR ANDREW LLOYD WEBBER.

TOM V/O: In his office in Troot, theatrical agent Jeremy Rent is having a very important meeting with Sir Andrew Lloyd Webber.

JEREMY: Sir Andrew, was it your idea to write *Bergerac: the Musical*?

SIR ANDREW: Oh yes, mine and Ben Elton's. It's something we always wanted to do and it's going to be even bigger than the one I did about cats. *Cats.*

VOICE ON INTERCOM: Dennis Waterman here to see you.

JEREMY: (INTO THE INTERCOM) Oh lovely, send him in.

SIR ANDREW: Well, it would be wonderful if we could get Dennis to play the part of Jim Bergerac.

DENNIS ENTERS, CARRYING A DOUGHNUT AROUND HIS WAIST LIKE AN ENORMOUS RUBBER RING.

DENNIS: Hello, I got you a doughnut.

JEREMY: Oh, thank you very much.

DENNIS STRUGGLES TO LIFT THE DOUGHNUT UP TO JEREMY; WE CUT TO JEREMY TAKING AN ORDINARY-SIZED DOUGHNUT.

DENNIS: (FRIGHTENED) Who is that man?

JEREMY: Oh, well this is Sir Andrew Lloyd Webber.

DENNIS: Oh yes: the brother of Julian Lloyd Webber, the famous cellist.

SIR ANDREW: Hello.

AN ENORMOUS HAND APPEARS IN SHOT, AND DENNIS DOES HIS BEST TO SHAKE IT.

SIR ANDREW: So, I've done *Bergerac: the Musical* and I'd love *you* to play the title role.

DENNIS: Doesn't Bergerac play Bergerac?

JEREMY: Oh, no, he's committed to *Midsomer Murders*.

DENNIS: (SHOCKED) He's committed murders? That is wrong and bad.

SIR ANDREW: Anyway, I'd be thrilled if you would consider it. This is the set for act one, Charlie Hungerford's house.

DENNIS GETS OFF HIS CHAIR AND WALKS OVER TO THE DESK, WHERE THERE IS A TINY MODEL OF A SET, ABOUT THE SIZE OF A DOLL'S HOUSE.

DENNIS: Oh. Let's have a look.

TWO ENORMOUS HANDS COME INTO SHOT, PICK DENNIS UP AND PLACE HIM INSIDE THE CARDBOARD SET.

DENNIS: Put me down.

SIR ANDREW: It's an exact replica of the one in the programme.

DENNIS: (EXCITED, LOOKING AROUND THE CARDBOARD ROOM) Yeah, this is great, you certainly wouldn't want it any bigger. So you want me to star in it . . . write the feem toon, sing the feem toon . . .

SIR ANDREW: No no, no ,no, no, I've written all the songs. Yes?

JEREMY: (STERNLY) Dennis . . .

DENNIS: (SINGING TO HIMSELF) I'm a policeman living in Jersey. Do do do do do do. I have a complicated relationship with my ex-wife. Do do do do do do. I drive an old red car, my boss has lost his hair, I'd be so good for *Bergerac the Musical* . . .

THERE IS A PAUSE.

SIR ANDREW: Well it's been wonderful to meet the both of you. Um, I do have one or two other people to see.

JEREMY: Yes . . .

ANDREW PICKS UP HIS MODEL SET – WE SEE DENNIS BEING THROWN ABOUT THE CARDBOARD ROOM.

DENNIS: Woooaaaahhhh! Woooaaaahhhh! Careful!

SIR ANDREW: I'm very sorry.

THE ENORMOUS HANDS REAPPEAR AND LIFT DENNIS OUT OF THE SET. WE THEN CUT TO JEREMY PUTTING A TINY, DENNIS-LIKE PLASTIC ACTION FIGURE ON THE DESK. IT TOPPLES OVER.

JEREMY: Alright Dennis, safe now.

BANK CLERK 4

EXT: BANK. THE USUAL OLD LADY DUTIFULLY PICKS UP A PIECE OF DOG EXCREMENT . . . AND TOSSES IT
TO A BEMUSED HOMELESS PERSON WHO IS SITTING ON THE PAVEMENT.

TOM V/O: To remain competitive, banks now offer a wide range of services, including
loans, insurance and for a small fee, they'll make love to your wife.

INT: BANK OFFICE. AN EMPLOYEE OF THE BANK COMES INTO THE OFFICE TO TALK TO CAROL.

MAN: (CALLING BEHIND HIM AS HE ENTERS) Yeah, that's Perry Keen outside. I'll call him back. (TO
CAROL, WARMLY) Hey, I'm not interrupting anything, am I? (CAROL STARES AT HIM, DEADPAN) Oh, I
heard you went to Prague, did you have a nice time? (CAROL SHRUGS) Right, well, you know
it's my leaving do on Thursday?

CAROL: Oh yeah?

MAN: Yeah, and, er, we're all going to go bowling and then have a bite to eat afterwards
at Bella Pasta?

CAROL: (DEADPAN) Oh, lovely.

MAN: Yeah, so we wondered whether you fancied coming, 'cause, er, we need to book the
table.

CAROL TURNS TO HER COMPUTER AND BEGINS TO TAP SOME KEYS.

CAROL: Computer says 'Will Melanie be there'?

MAN: (BRIGHTLY) Yeah, yeah she's coming.

CAROL TYPES AGAIN. THERE IS A PAUSE.

CAROL: Computer says 'No'.

SHE COUGHS AT HIM.

MAN: (AWKWARDLY) Right, well if you, if you change your mind, then . . .

HE LEAVES. CAROL WATCHES HIM GO, AND THEN WHISPERS AFTER HIM.

CAROL: I love you.

To remain competitive, banks now offer a wide range of services, including loans, insurance and for a small fee, they'll make love to your wife.

Homophobe!

DAFFYD – LESBIAN WEDDING

EXT: A COUNTRY COTTAGE. DAFFYD APPEARS, WALKING DOWN THE LANE.

TOM V/O: Like many people in Britain, every other Wednesday I go gay. Daffyd Thomas is a full-time gay and is on his way to his local pub for a celebration.

THE LOCAL BAKER WALKS OVER TO DAFFYD WITH A BASKET OF BREAD.

BAKER: (FRIENDLY) Hello Daffyd, fancy a bun?

DAFFYD: Homophobe!

INT: PUB. MYFANWY AND ANOTHER WOMAN, RHIANNON, ARE HUGGING EACH OTHER JOYFULLY, DRESSED AS BRIDE AND GROOM.

MYFANWY: You've made me the happiest girl in the world.

RHIANNON: I love you, Myfanwy.

MYFANWY: And I love you too, Rhiannon.

THE OTHER PEOPLE IN THE PUB CHEER. DAFFYD ENTERS AND COUGHS TO ANNOUNCE HIS PRESENCE.

MYFANWY: (HAPPILY) Oh Daffyd, you made it. We didn't know if you were coming.

DAFFYD: Yeah sorry I'm late – of course, I couldn't come to the church service.

MYFANWY: Why not?

DAFFYD: I am a gay, I wouldn't be welcome.

VICAR: But I'm gay and I was performing a gay marriage, of course you would be welcome.

VERGER: You never know, Daffyd, if you met a nice young man maybe the Vicar would marry you?

I don't know, gay marriage, adoption, what's wrong with just sitting at home in front of the television, getting moist every time Sandy Toksvig comes on?

Welcome t
CROESO
LLANDEWI

DAFFYD: No thank you, Verger, if I get married it will be to a woman into a life of misery and repression.

VERGER: Please yourself, dear.

MYFANWY: Anyway, come and meet my friends. Everyone, this is Daffyd.

DAFFYD: Hello, yes, Daffyd Thomas, the only gay in the village, yeah.

No thank you, Verger, if I get married it will be to a woman into a life of misery and repression.

MYFANWY: Actually Daffyd, we were hoping to have a little word with you.

RHIANNON: Yes, we're applying for adoption and wonder if you'll be our referee?

DAFFYD: (SHOCKED AND DISGUSTED) Ugh, but you're two great minge munchers!

MYFANWY: (PUZZLED) Yes . . .

DAFFYD: (POMPOUSLY) Well you can't be bringing up kids, it's not right.

RHIANNON: Oh, well I'm sorry you feel that way.

DAFFYD: I don't know, gay marriage, adoption, what's wrong with just sitting at home in front of the television, getting moist every time Sandy Toksvig comes on?

RHIANNON: Well we've moved on a bit since then, love.

DAFFYD: Anyway, what do lesbians do exactly, I mean, I don't get it.

DAFFYD MIMES HOLES WITH HIS INDEX FINGERS AND THUMBS, AND LOOKS CONFUSED. AN ATTRACTIVE LADY WHO HAS BEEN LISTENING STANDS UP.

LADY IN PUB: We do all sorts of things.

DAFFYD: Sorry, I was talking to the lesbians.

LADY IN PUB: I am a lesbian.

DAFFYD: What? You can't be, you're far too good looking.

LADY IN PUB: What are you talking about?

DAFFYD: Well I just thought it was the ones that couldn't get boyfriends.

RHIANNON: Oh piss off, you stupid little poof!

DAFFYD: Oh, how dare you! I will not tolerate homophobia in this village, good day!
(CALLING BACK OVER HIS SHOULDER) Dirty fat lezzers!

LOU AND ANDY — PARIS

INT: ANDY IS IN THE BATH. LOU SITS BESIDE THE TUB, REACHING IN TO SCRUB ANDY'S BACK.

TOM V/O: In Herby, Andy Pipkin is enjoying his annual bath.

LOU: Right, now I've planned the route to Chessington, it's really just straight down the A217. So if we get our skates on, we'll be on the log flume by lunchtime.

ANDY: I don't want to go.

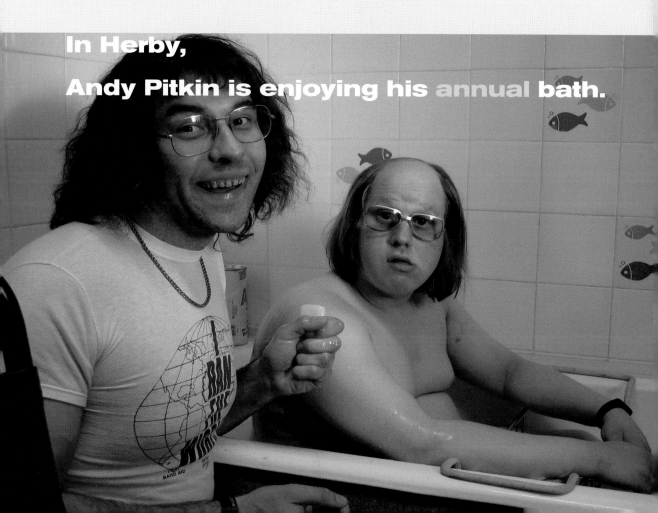

In Herby,

Andy Pitkin is enjoying his annual bath.

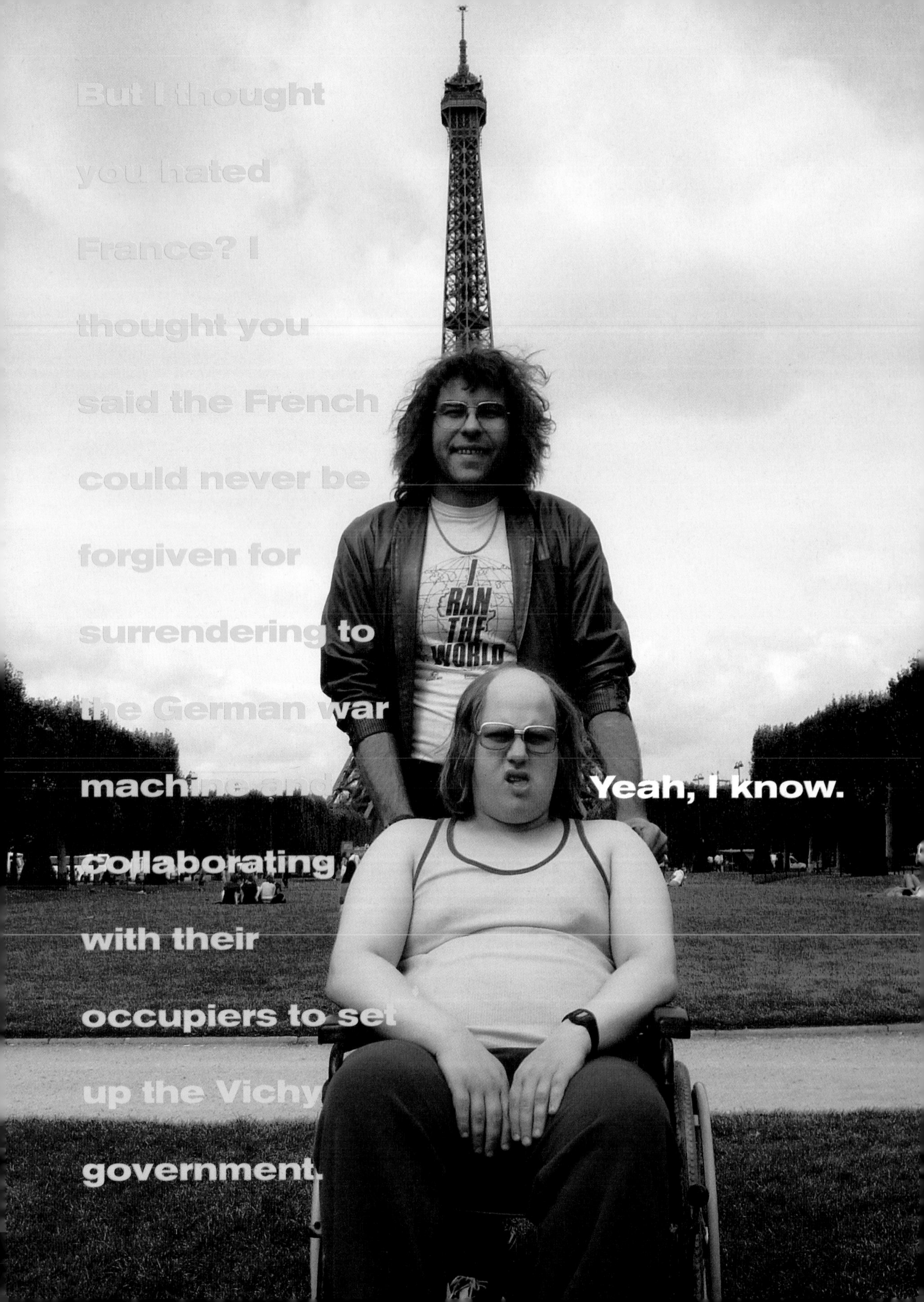
But I thought you hated France? I thought you said the French could never be forgiven for surrendering to the German war machine and collaborating with their occupiers to set up the Vichy government.
Yeah, I know.
I
RAN
THE
WORLD

LOU: But you've been going on non stop about it for weeks. Chessington World of Adventures this, Chessington World of Adventures that . . .

ANDY: Yeah, I know.

LOU: Well where do you want to go instead?

ANDY: France.

LOU: France?

ANDY: Yeah.

LOU: But I thought you hated France? I thought you said the French could never be forgiven for surrendering to the German war machine and collaborating with their occupiers to set up the Vichy government.

ANDY: Yeah, I know.

LOU: Chessington it is, then.

ANDY: I wanna go France.

LOU: (MUTTERING TO HIMSELF) Christ of a thousand years.

EXT: PARIS. WE SEE A LONG SHOT OF THE EIFFEL TOWER. IT IS A BEAUTIFUL DAY, AND LOU IS PUSHING ANDY THROUGH THE GARDENS IN FRONT OF THE TOWER.

ANDY: I wanna go Chessington.

LOU STOPS, TURNS THE WHEELCHAIR ROUND, AND BEGINS TO WALK BACK THE OTHER WAY, OUT OF SHOT.

TOM V/O: And so we end our trip round Little Britain. If you have enjoyed this evening's programme, you might like to travel back in time half an hour and watch it again. Good die.

Carol Beer's Page By Carol Beer

Hello, my name is Carol Beer.
This is my page written by me, Carol Beer.

When people pass by my desk they often comment
about my zany/wacky screensavers that go with my madcap personality.

Here are six of my designs,
which I hope will keep you entertained for a little while.
I hope you agree with me that they are all wicked!!

12

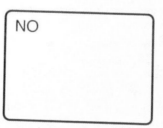

Well readers I do hope that you had as much fun looking at my designs as I had designing them. I'm off now to stare into space for a bit. Bye!!!!!!

EPISODE

TOM V/O: Britain, Britain, Britain. I love Britain so much that every day I sacrifice a child in honour of it, so thank the Lord – who, incidentally, is British – for the great things he has brought to this land: Take A Break, Spearmint Rhino and Findus Crispy Pancakes. But also let us give thanks for the people of Britain, and it is them whom we'll be doing looking at today. Boogaloo!

LOU AND ANDY — ANDY'S DATE

EXT: A PARK. LOU IS PUSHING ANDY ALONG IN HIS WHEELCHAIR.

TOM V/O: Today, Lou has arranged for Andy to go on a blind date. I went on a blind date once with a border collie. Nothing came of it, but we stay in touch.

ANDY IS TUCKING INTO A BAG OF CHIPS AS LOU WHEELS HIM ALONG.

LOU: Can I have one of them chips?

ANDY: No.

LOU: Please?

ANDY: No, should have got your own.

LOU: But I only had enough for one.

ANDY: Yeah, I know.

LOU: (TO HIDE HIS DISAPPOINTMENT) Well it doesn't matter, 'cause I don't want any chips now anyway.

ANDY IMMEDIATELY THROWS HIS CHIPS ONTO THE FLOOR.

ANDY: Nor do I.

THERE IS A PAUSE, BEFORE LOU CHANGES THE SUBJECT.

LOU: So, are you excited about this date?

ANDY: Yeah. What date?

LOU: The date, I fixed you up with a date with a lady.

ANDY: Yeah, I know.

LOU: Now, her name is Francesca, and I said we'd meet her at the steps at five sharp. Ooh, she's early, hello Francesca, how are you?

WE SEE A NICE YOUNG WOMAN SITTING IN HER WHEELCHAIR, WAITING. SHE SMILES BRIGHTLY AS LOU AND ANDY
APPROACH.

FRANCESCA: Very well, thanks.

LOU: Oh that is good. Now, this is Andy who I was telling you about.

FRANCESCA: (SMILING) Hello, Andy.

Well it doesn't matter, 'cause I don't want any chips now anyway.

Nor do I.

I don't want that one

WITHOUT LOOKING AT HER, ANDY WAVES HIS ARM IN HER GENERAL DIRECTION.

ANDY: I don't want that one.

LOU LOOKS EMBARRASSED.

LOU: Why not?

ANDY: She's in a wheelchair.

LOU: (EMBARASSED) Yes, I know she's in a wheelchair.

ANDY: I don't like it.

LOU: (TRYING TO SMOOTH THINGS OVER) Well, it's early days, I'll leave you two alone, er, you don't need me here playing raspberry. Alright, now have a lovely time.

LOU WALKS OFF.

FRANCESCA: (STILL TRYING HER BEST TO BE FRIENDLY) Well Andy, I've heard a lot about you.

WITHOUT LOOKING AT HER, ANDY GETS OUT OF WHEELCHAIR, STANDS BEHIND FRANCESCA'S WHEELCHAIR AND PUSHES HER SMARTLY DOWN THE STEPS BEFORE SITTING BACK DOWN IN HIS CHAIR. WE SEE HER BUMP DOWN THE STEPS AND OFF INTO THE DISTANCE AT SPEED. WE THEN CUT TO LOU WALKING ALONG, HAPPILY – AND FRANCESCA SCREAMING AS SHE RACES PAST. LOU RUNS AFTER HER.

VICKY POLLARD – BOYFRIEND

EXT: A CHILDREN'S PLAYGROUND. VICKY'S FRIENDS ARE SITTING ON ONE OF THE CLIMBING FRAMES, SMOKING AND TEXTING ON THEIR MOBILES.

TOM V/O: In Darkly Noone, Vicky Pollard's gang are keen to get on with their day's robbing.

VICKY'S FRIEND 1: Where is Vicky, she was so supposed to be here by now?

VICKY'S FRIEND 2: She's got that black boyfriend now ain't she, she's probably with 'im.

VICKY'S FRIEND 3: She has well changed since she's gone with that Jermaine.

WE SEE VICKY APPEAR WITH HER ARM AROUND THE SHOULDERS OF HER NEW

BOYFRIEND, JERMAINE. SHE WALKS TOWARDS HER FRIENDS.

VICKY'S FRIEND 1: Er, take your time why don't you.

VICKY'S FRIEND2: Alright Vicky, where've you been?

VICKY: (IN A THICK JAMAICAN ACCENT) No but yeah but no but yeah but no because of somethin' happen I don't even know nothing about so like shut up and don't go giving me evil because me got like me man Jermaine now and we just been like round the back of the water slides making baby.

VICKY'S FRIEND 3: So you coming robbing down Woollies with us later or what?

VICKY: Me don't know me think about just hanging with me man Jermaine and be cooking up some chicken and rice and peas for him but yeah but no but yeah because it's up to Jermaine now because me like his bitch now so Jermaine what say you?

JERMAINE: (IN A VERY POSH, PUBLIC SCHOOL ACCENT) Well I don't really know, Victoria, I'm just happy to go with the flow.

VICKY: Me man has spoken, Woollies it is . . . Ras clart.

EPISODE Six

Me don't know me think about just hanging with me man Jermaine and be cooking up some chicken and rice and peas for him but yeah but no but yeah because it's up to Jermaine now because me like his bitch now so Jermaine what say you?

Me man has spoken, Woollies it is . . . Ras clart.

I think I've got a

TWO LADIES IN RESTAURANT 1

INT: RESTAURANT. TWO WELL-OFF YOUNG LADIES ARE ORDERING LUNCH.

TOM V/O: Meaning while at this restaurant in Chafe.

RACHEL: . . . and a rocket salad, thank you. (TURNING TO HER FRIEND) So, you still haven't heard from Alistair?

NICOLA: No, I think he's gone back to that Sasha.

RACHEL: Sorry. Well . . . I've been wanting to introduce you to my friend Jonathan.

NICOLA: Oh yes . . .

RACHEL: Mm, he's single, works in the City, he's got a lovely apartment in the Docklands actually.

picture of him.

NICOLA: Ooh, so he's doing well for himself.

RACHEL: Yes, he's just brought a place in Provence.

NICOLA: Ooh, sounds wonderful.

RACHEL BEGINS TO LOOK IN HER BAG.

RACHEL: I think I've got a picture of him.

SHE PASSES HER FRIEND A POLAROID PHOTO. THE SECOND LADY LOOKS VERY PLEASED.

NICOLA: Oh, he looks lovely.

WE SEE THE POLAROID, WHICH IS OF A NAKED MAN PHOTOGRAPHED FROM THE WAIST DOWN.

REVEREND JESSIE KING

EXT: CHURCH. WE SEE A SIGN OUTSIDE WHICH READS: 'ST. JESUS'S CHURCH – OPEN MON–SAT 10-6 – CLOSED SUNDAYS'.

TOM V/O: Christianity is one of the most popular religions in Britain, with over eighty members.

INT: CHURCH. THE ORGANIST IS ADDRESSING THE CONGREGATION.

ORGANIST: Please be seated. Now as you know, the Reverend Hartley is on an exchange trip to Harlem in New York, so they've sent their Reverend here to take the service this week. Now, I imagine he's a little nervous, so I want you all to make him feel very welcome. His name is Reverend Jessie King.

THE REVEREND JESSIE KING APPEARS AT THE BACK OF THE CHURCH, HOLLERING IN A LOUD AMERICAN ACCENT.

REV JESSIE KING: Hallelujah! I . . . is from the ghetto! *You* . . . is from the ghetto. We is *all* from the ghetto . . . But how we gonna get out the ghetto? I tell you how we's gonna get out the ghetto, we is gonna *fight the power*, fight the power, fight the power. (TURNING TO HOLD HIS MICROPHONE TO A NERVOUS-LOOKING MIDDLE-AGED WOMAN) What we gonna do, momma?

WOMAN IN CONGREGATION: (UNCERTAINLY) Fight the power, perhaps?

JESSIE TOUCHES HER HEAD AND PUSHES HER BACK, AS IF HEALING HER.

REV JESSIE KING: (SOFTLY) Praise the Lord. (SHOUTS) Hallelujah! Say 'Praise be to Jesus'!

CONGREGATION: (AWKWARDLY AND QUITE QUIETLY) Praise be to Jesus.

REV JESSIE KING: (HOLLERING) Say 'Praise be to the Lord'!

CONGREGATION: Praise be to the Lord.

REV JESSIE KING: Say 'Hi de hi de hi'.

CONGREGATION: Hi de hi de hi.

REV JESSIE KING: Say 'Ho de ho de ho'.

CONGREGATION: Ho de ho de ho.

REV JESSIE KING: Go go go to the holiday rock. Praise the Lord, amen!

CONGREGATION: Amen.

REV JESSIE KING: And now it is time to call upon Lord Jesus to come amongst us today and heal the sick and the lame. Anyone here who can't walk? (SILENCE. HE MIMES WALKING BACKWARDS AND FORWARDS) Who can't do that? Anyone here . . . with leprosy, any lepers in the house? (SILENCE. HE ADDRESS A NORMAL-LOOKING MAN IN THE FRONT ROW) Brother, what be your sickness?

MAN IN CONGREGATION: I'm fine, it's just a slight cough.

REV JESSIE KING: Come and join me, brother, Jesus will cure you. Excuse me while I talk in tongues for a moment. (HE BEGINS TO BABBLE FOR SEVERAL SECONDS, BEFORE SLAPPING THE MAN ROUND THE FACE) Well?

MAN IN CONGREGATION: (TOUCHING HIS THROAT, EMBARRASSED) Still a bit tickly.

JESSIE HANDS A PACKET OF LOZENGES TO THE MAN.

REV JESSIE KING: Try these. He can walk! Hallelujah, praise the Lord!

HALLELUJAH!

...is from the ghetto!

Oh, well you know me and

MARJORIE DAWES/FATFIGHTERS —
ENGAGEMENT PARTY

INT: THE FATFIGHTERS MEETING ROOM. THERE IS A LAVISH BUFFET LAID OUT ON TABLES, AND A CAKE THAT IS
DECORATED WITH THE WORDS: 'CONGRATULATIONS PAT AND PAUL'.

TOM V/O: There is no greater shame in Britain than being fat. I had a fat son who,
naturally, I gave up for adoption. He's written to me several times saying he's lost
weight and would like to meet up but I'm not interested.

MARJORIE WALKS INTO THE ROOM AND SEES ALL OF THE FOOD.

MARJORIE: What the hell's all this?

PAUL: Oh, well you know me and Pat have gotten engaged.

MARJORIE: Yeah . . .

PAUL: Well we've booked the hall to have a party afterwards.

PAT: We've been setting up all afternoon.

Pat have gotten engaged.

MARJORIE: Looks cheap. OK, so, let's start with the weigh . . . Hang on a minute, I don't remember getting my invitation.

PAT: (AWKWARDLY) Oh, no, well it was just, you know, close friends and family.

MARJORIE: Right, (ADDRESSING ONE OF THE OTHER MEMBERS) you're going are you?

FATFIGHTER 1: Oh yes.

MARJORIE: You?

FATFIGHTER 2: Yeah.

MARJORIE: What about you, you going?

TANIA: Yes.

MARJORIE: What about you Meera, you going?

MEERA: Yes.

MARJORIE: Sorry? Do it again.

Why don't you just stick shit through my letter box, huh?

MEERA: Yes.

MARJORIE: Do it again.

MERA: Yes.

MARJORIE: Now, do it again.

MEERA: (FRUSTRATED) Yes, yes, yes, yes.

MARJORIE: (TO THE GROUP, PRETENDING TO BE PUZZLED) Was that a yes or . . . we'll never know, we need an interpreter really. And all this food's for the party is it?

PAUL: Erm, yeah.

MARJORIE: Well what are these supposed to be?

PAT: Vol-au-vents.

MARJORIE: Vol-au-vents? Come on, we did vol-au-vents last week, am I wasting my time? They are absolute calorie hot spots.

MARJORIE PICKS UP THE PLATE OF VOL-AU-VENTS AND PUTS THEM IN THE BIN.

PAT: Marjorie!

MARJORIE: I'm only thinking of you, Pat, you know you've got your wedding day coming up. I want to see you get down to a size thirty. (HOLDING ANOTHER PLATE UP) What are these?

PAT: Mini chipolatas.

MARJORIE: Why don't you just stick shit through my letter box, huh? (THROWS IT AWAY) And what the hell is this supposed to be?

TANIA: Oh I made it, it's Banoffee pie.

MARJORIE: (IN A DEEP VOICE, MIMICKING TANIA) 'Oh I made it, it's Banoffee pie'. You, Tania, are playing Russian roulade with these people's lives here, because if one of these fatties has a single bite of this they could drop down dead. Shame on you, Tania, boo, hiss, boo.

MARJORIE PUTS THE PIE IN HER OWN HANDBAG.

PAUL: (EXASPERATED) We're just trying to have a party, Marjorie.

THERE IS A PAUSE.

MARJORIE: (KINDLY, SMILING) Yeah you're right, what am I thinking. Let's not worry about FatFighters today, have a lovely time and I wish you all the best for the future.

ON HER WAY OUT, MARJORIE STOPS, VIOLENTLY OVERTURNS ONE OF THE TABLES LADEN WITH FOOD, AND LEAVES THE ROOM.

Yeah you're right, what am I thinking. Let's not worry about FatFighters today, have a lovely time and I wish you all the best for the future.

KENNY CRAIG — STAGE SHOW 1

EXT: A SMALL THEATRE. KENNY IS PUTTING UP ONE OF HIS POSTERS ON THE WALL OUTSIDE. IT READS 'TONIGHT! KENNY CRAIG'S HYPNOTIC LAUGHTER SHOW'.

TOM V/O: Today stage hypnotist Kenny Craig's three-date national tour has arrived in Snitch.

KENNY CRAIG (OFFSTAGE): Ladies and gentlemen, will you please welcome hypnotist extraordinaire, Kennnnyyyyy Craiiiigggg.

KENNY WALKS ONTO THE STAGE, SMILING, AND ALMOST IMMEDIATELY BEGINS TO HYPNOTIZE THE CROWD.

KENNY CRAIG: Thank you very much, thank you. Thank you very much indeed and welcome to the show. Look into my eyes, look into my eyes, the eyes, the eyes, not around the eyes, don't look around the eyes, look into my eyes (CLICKS HIS FINGERS) you're under. In one hour's time I will click my fingers and you will all believe that you have witnessed a superb hypnotic comedy show that was excellent value for money, much better than Paul McKenna and that new bloke Derren what's-his-name, and you will tell all your friends . . . hold the thought.

THE AUDIENCE STARE BLANKLY AHEAD, HYPNOTIZED. KENNY CREEPS OVER TO A CHAIR ONSTAGE, PICKS UP A BOOK – Bravo Two Zero – AND STARTS TO READ.

In one hour's time I will click my fingers and you will all believe that you have witnessed a superb hypnotic comedy show that was excellent value for money, much better than Paul McKenna and that new bloke Derren what's-his-name, and you will tell all your friends . . . hold the thought.

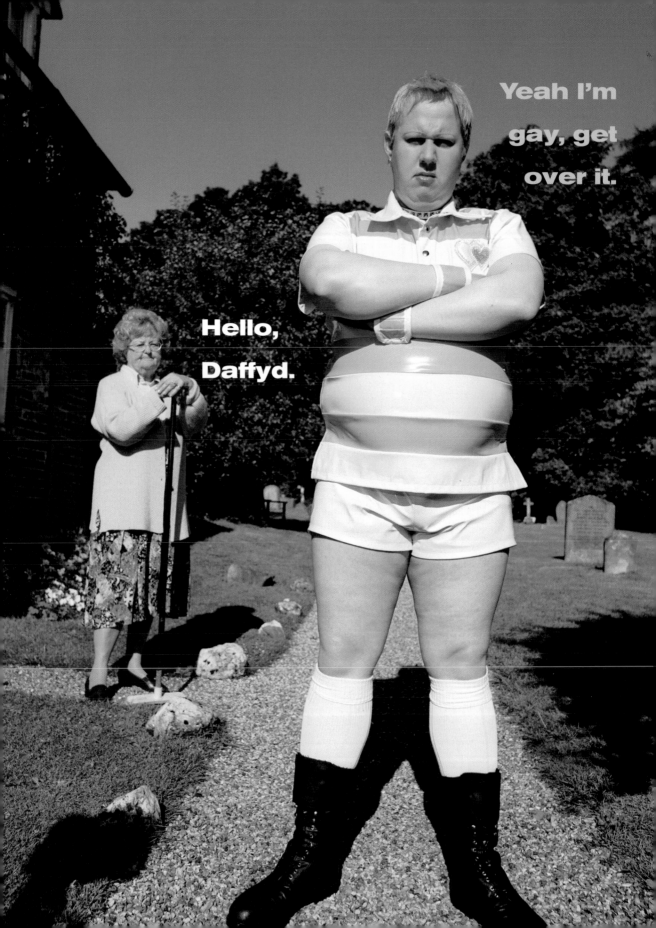

DAFFYD – RUGBY (BBC3 ONLY)

EXT: DAFFYD IS WALKING THROUGH THE VILLAGE, WEARING A PINK AND WHITE STRIPED RUGBY KIT..

TOM V/O: With this afternoon's Welsh Gay Rugby league match over, local fruit Daffyd Thomas is heading off to the pub.

DAFFYD WALKS PAST A LADY WHO IS DOING THE GARDENING.

LADY: Hello, Daffyd.

DAFFYD: (CROSSLY) Yeah I'm gay, get over it.

INT: PUB. MYFANWY IS SERVING A DRINK TO FARMER HUGHES, WHO IS SITTING AT THE BAR.

MYFANWY: There you go, Farmer Hughes.

FARMER HUGHES: Thank you, my love.

DAFFYD WALKS INTO THE PUB.

DAFFYD: Ten Bacardi and Cokes, please

MYFANWY: Oh, coming right up.

DAFFYD: In you come, fellows.

A TEAM OF RUGBY PLAYERS WALK INTO THE PUB. THEY ARE ALL WEARING A BLUE AND WHITE STRIPED KIT.

RUGBY PLAYER: Come on, lads. Get in here.

MYFANWY: Oh, so who are all this lot, then?

DAFFYD: Oh, they're from Bangor.

MYFANWY: Oh right.

DAFFYD: Yes, Llandewi Breffi played them today in the Gay Rugby league.

MYFANWY: Oh, who won?

DAFFYD: (MEEKLY) Bangor, ninety-six–nil.

MYFANWY: Oh, so what's happened to all our lot then?

DAFFYD: Oh no, it's just me you see, as you know I am the only gay in the village.

RUGBY PLAYER 1: Funny you say that, I was here last week, you couldn't move for cock.

RUGBY PLAYER 2: Yeah, it was non stop bum fun.

DAFFYD: (RATTLED) No, you're quite wrong.

FARMER HUGHES: Well I'd loved to have played but I never heard nothing about it.

DAFFYD: Yes, but this was a gay team for gays.

FARMER HUGHES: Well, I've tugged the odd todger in my time.

DAFFYD: (TRYING TO SHUT HIM UP) Yes, thank you, Farmer Hughes.

A MINER WALKS OVER.

MINER: Excuse me, excuse me, I'm a good winger.

DAFFYD: Yes but you're married.

MINER: But I'm always cottaging.

DAFFYD: (INCREASINGLY SHOCKED) Well what about your wife?

MINER: (MATTER-OF-FACTLY) Oh she don't mind, she's bi-curious herself.

DAFFYD: Disgusting.

Well where are you going?

As far away from here as possible, to a place where gay people are not welcome, where I am the only one.

THE VILLAGE BAKER COMES OVER TO JOIN THE CONVERSATION.

BAKER: So which toilets do you use then?

MINER: The one in the park, of course.

BAKER: Oh yes, I thought I'd seen you through the glory hole.

POSTMAN: I think I'm a bit old now for rugby but I'm a big fan of fisting.

DAFFYD: (CROSSLY) Is there nobody in this pub who isn't gay?

POLICEMAN: Well, I indulged in mutual masturbation when I was younger, does that count?

DAFFYD TURNS TO AN OLD LOLLIPOP MAN.

DAFFYD: What about you Mr Jenkins?

MR JENKINS: Oh, well since I retired I've discovered the joys of rimming.

DAFFYD: Right, that is it, I've had it with this village, I'm leaving, goodbye everybody.

MYFANWY: Well where are you going?

DAFFYD: As far away from here as possible, to a place where gay people are not welcome, where I am the only one.

MYFANWY: Where?

DAFFYD THOMAS: I got two uncles in San Francisco, I'm gonna go there.

HE LEAVES TRIUMPHANTLY.

EPISODE six

DAFFYD — GAY LIAISON OFFICER (BBC1 ONLY)

TOM V/O: Daffyd Thomas is gay. Gay used to be such a lovely word, one could go to a gay bar, meet a gay man and have gay sex and there were no homosexual connotations whatsoever.

DAFFYD APPROACHES LLANDEWI POLICE STATION, A POLICEMAN IS LEAVING THE STATION.

POLICEMAN: Hello Daffyd

DAFFYD: (PRODUCING MEGAPHONE FROM BEHIND HIS BACK, AND HOLDING IT TO HIS MOUTH) Love is not a crime.

WE CUT TO INTERIOR OF THE POLICE STATION

SUPERINTENDANT GRIFFITHS: (ON THE PHONE) Mrs Evans? It's Superintendent Griffiths. Good news; we've found your bucket. Good day.

WE CUT TO EXTERIOR OF POLICE STATION, DAFFYD ENTERING THE BUILDING.

GRIFFITHS: Hello

DAFFYD: Good afternoon, Daffyd Thomas, the only gay in the village.

GRIFFITHS: Ah yes, so you'd like to join the police force?

DAFFYD: Not particularly, my restart officer sent me, but I know you don't allow gays in the police so I might as well leave now. Good day.

(TURNS TO LEAVE)

GRIFFITHS: Oh no, no, no, that's not true at all. No, the police (POINTS TO SIGN) is an equal opportunities employer. In fact we've just taken on a Sheikh officer, and a lady in a wheelchair.

DAFFYD: Humph, political correctness gone mad.

GRIFFITHS: We're actually looking for a gay liaison officer.

DAFFYD: How dare you, I've never had a gay liaison in my life!

GRIFFITHS: It's someone who can relate to the gay community, who they can interface with.

DAFFYD: No, I'm not really in to face, I'm more in to bum.

GRIFFITHS: What I mean is it's someone who's gay who can go to the bars and clubs and talk to the gay community in their own language.

DAFFYD: They have their own language?

GRIFFITHS: It's a figure of speech.

DAFFYD: Where are all these gay clubs anyway?

GRIFFITHS: Well, there's a thriving gay district in Merthyr. I say district, it's more of a gay road really.

DAFFYD: The road is gay?

GRIFFITHS: There are a couple of bars, a club and a gay restaurant it's very popular.

How dare you,
I've never had a gay liaison in my life!

DAFFYD: A gay restaurant, so the food there is gay? The napkins? How does this work?

GRIFFITHS: (LEANING FORWARD) Do you want this job or not?

DAFFYD: (LEANING FORWARD) Do I get to wear the uniform?

GRIFFITHS: Yes.

DAFFYD: I'll take it.

WE CUT TO EXTERIOR SHOT OF VILLAGE, DAFFYD APPEARS DRESSED IN HIS NEW POLICE UNIFORM, A SKIN TIGHT, SHORT-SLEEVED, BLACK LATEX TOP AND A BLACK SHINY JOCK STRAP WITH A MINUTE POLICEMAN'S HAT ON HIS HEAD. DAFFYD PASSES TWO OLD LADIES WHO TURN TO GREET HIM.

DAFFYD: Evening all.

THE STUNNED OLD LADIES WATCH HIM PASS AND WE SEE DAFFYD'S BARE BUTTOCKS AS HE WALKS AWAY.

KENNY CRAIG – STAGE SHOW 2

KENNY CRAIG IS SITTING ON STAGE, ENGROSSED IN HIS BOOK. THE AUDIENCE ARE STILL IN A TRANCE. AFTER A WHILE, KENNY FINALLY PUTS Bravo Two Zero DOWN AND LOOKS PLEASED WITH HIMSELF FOR HAVING WORKED SOMETHING OUT.

KENNY CRAIG: (TO HIMSELF) Oh, so he's in the *army*. Ha!

SUDDENLY REALIZING THAT HE IS STILL UP ON STAGE, HE STANDS UP AND BRINGS THE AUDIENCE OUT OF THEIR TRANCE.

KENNY CRAIG: Oh yeah, three – two – one . . . You're back in the room. (APPLAUSE) Thank you, thank you very much indeed, thank you. You've been a great audience, thank you very much. Don't forget to tell your friends, goodnight.

EPISODE six

Did he have longer hair?

TWO LADIES IN RESTAURANT 2

INT: RESTAURANT. A WAITRESS IS BRINGING DRINKS OVER TO THE SAME TWO LADIES AS BEFORE.

RACHEL: (QUIETLY) Oh she's taking bloody ages with those drinks. (THE WAITRESS ARRIVES) Oh, thank you very much. (TO HER FRIEND) Oh, it's a shame about Jonathan.

NICOLA: Oh I know, he just talked about himself the whole night.

RACHEL: (BRIGHTENING) Well, there's a good friend of mine, Rupert, have you met Rupert?

NICOLA: No, I don't think I have.

RACHEL: He's more of a friend of Simon's actually, he's just split up with his girlfriend.

NICOLA: Oh, what's he like?

RACHEL: Well, he's lovely, very good looking, he's an architect. I've got a picture of him I think . . . Oh yes . . .

SHE REACHES INTO HER BAG AND PULLS OUT A POLAROID OF A MAN FROM THE WAIST DOWN, WITH HIS PENIS POKING OUT OF THE ZIP OF HIS TROUSERS.

THE SECOND LADY LOOKS AT THE PHOTO ADMIRINGLY.

NICOLA: Looks familiar.

RACHEL: He was at Harriet's wedding.

NICOLA: Did he have longer hair?

HARVEY AND JANE – THE WEDDING

INT: CHURCH. HARVEY AND JANE ARE STANDING IN FRONT OF THE VICAR, READY TO MAKE THEIR MARRIAGE VOWS.

TOM V/O: Before you can get divorced in Britain, you need to get married. For Harvey and Jane the big day has finally arrived.

VICAR: And now it is time for Jane and Harvey to make their wedding vows. Do you, Harvey Tobias Jerome Pincher, take Jane Louise Edwards to be your lawful wedded wife?

HARVEY: (SMILING) Bitty.

VICAR: I'm sorry?

HARVEY: Bitty

VICAR: (PROMPTING HARVEY IN A WHISPER) No, it's 'I do'.

TURNING TO LOOK AT HIS MOTHER, IN THE FRONT ROW.

HARVEY: I know but I hungry, I want bitty.

CELIA: Oh come on Harvey, I fed you on the way here.

GERALD: We're eating in an hour.

HARVEY'S GRANDMA: Do you want me to go?

CELIA : No no no, Mummy . . .

CELIA GETS UP AND LEADS HARVEY TO A SEAT BY THE ALTAR. CELIA SITS DOWN AND HARVEY BEGINS TO BREAST-FEED WHILE THE VICAR AND JANE LOOK ON, HORRIFIED.

CELIA: (TO THE VICAR) I'm terribly sorry, it's a lovely service. Carry on.

VICAR : Do you erm . . . erm, take this woman to be your lawful wedded wife?

HARVEY BREAKS OFF FROM FEEDING TO TURN AND SPEAK TO THE VICAR.

HARVEY: I do.

VICAR: And do you, Jane Louise Edwards, take this . . . (THERE IS A LONG PAUSE) *man*, to be your lawful wedded husband?

JANE LOOKS OVER TO HER PARENTS QUESTIONINGLY. JANE'S DAD IS SHAKING HIS HEAD SLOWLY, STUNNED.

JANE: Erm . . . I do.

VICAR: I declare you man and wife. You may kiss the bride.

HARVEY GETS UP WITH A MILK MOUSTACHE AND WALKS OVER TO JANE. HE WIPES HIS MOUTH AND LEANS IN TO KISS HER. AFTER RECOILING SLIGHTLY, JANE LEANS IN AND KISSES HIM, SOMEWHAT RELUCTANTLY.

EPISODE *six*

DENNIS WATERMAN — STAR WARS

INT: OFFICE. JEREMY IS SITTING AT HIS DESK, MAKING A PHONE CALL.

TOM V/O: In Troot, theatrical agent Jeremy Rent is working hard for his stellar list of clients.

JEREMY: Hello, this is a message for the editor of *OK!* magazine, Jeremy Rent here. My client Liza Goddard has just had a new loft extension and I'm offering you an exclusive on it for thirty pounds. I look forward to hearing from you, goodbye.

RECEPTIONIST'S VOICE: Dennis Waterman here to see you.

JEREMY: Lovely, send him in.

TINY DENNIS WATERMAN WALKS IN, SHAKING A NORMAL-SIZED UMBRELLA.

DENNIS: Hello. It's raining cats and dogs out there.

JEREMY: Hello Dennis, let me take that from you. (HE TAKES HOLD OF A TINY UMBRELLA) You sound a bit bunged up

DENNIS: Yeah, bit of a cold.

JEREMY: Here, have a tissue.

DENNIS: Have you not got any man-sized?

JEREMY: No.

DENNIS IS GIVEN AN ENORMOUS TISSUE THE SIZE OF A BED SHEET. HE BLOWS HIS NOSE, LOOKS INTO THE TISSUE AND THEN QUICKLY LOOKS AWAY, DISGUSTED.

JEREMY: Now, I've had a call from George Lucas . . .

DENNIS: (EXCITED) Oh, the man who done *Howard the Duck*.

JEREMY: Yes . . . and *Star Wars*.

DENNIS: (UNIMPRESSED) Oh, he done that as well.

JEREMY: Anyway, he's making a brand new *Star Wars* film and he wants you to be Obi-Wan's cousin, Kenneth Kenobi.

DENNIS: Oh that's nice, so they want me to star in it, write the feem toon, sing the feem toon?

JEREMY: No, no, they've already got their own music.

DENNIS: (HUFFILY) Tell him to get stuffed.

JEREMY: Dennis, *Star Wars* is a very big deal and can make you an awful lot of money, they'd even make an action figure of you like this . . .

Man, that's good . . .

JEREMY HANDS A TINY ACTION FIGURE ACROSS THE DESK; WE CUT TO DENNIS TAKING HOLD OF A HUGE STORMTROOPER.

DENNIS: Ooh, life-size.

JEREMY: Well?

DENNIS: (SINGING SOFTLY TO HIMSELF) In a galaxy far away in space, de do do do do do, the bad men are taking over space, de do do do do do . . .

JEREMY: Dennis!

DENNIS: (STILL SINGING, BREAKING INTO THE *MINDER* THEME TUNE) I've got a good idea, just you keep me near, I'll be so good for the Rebel Alliance. (SPEAKING) It obviously will sound a bit better on the day, still a bit snotty.

JEREMY PASSES A SMALL NASAL INHALER STICK TO DENNIS.

JEREMY: Here, try this.

WE SEE DENNIS HOLDING A GIANT INHALER ALMOST AS BIG AS HE IS. HE INHALES DEEPLY.

DENNIS: Man, that's good . . .

EPISODE **six**

BUBBLES DEVERE – BOARDROOM

INT: HILL GRANGE HEALTH SPA. MR HUTTON IS ADDRESSING A MEETING OF THE BOARD.

TOM V/O: It's half past Wilhelm, and at this health spa Mr Hutton is taking an important meeting. Meetings are when people who need to meet meet and have a meeting.

BUBBLES MAKES A GRAND ENTRANCE WHILE THE MEETING IS IN PROGRESS. SHE IS COMPLETELY NAKED, COVERED IN AN ALL-BODY MUD-PACK.

BUBBLES: Mr Hutton, a word.

MR HUTTON: Mrs DeVere, I'm just in the middle of a meeting.

BUBBLES: What is this thing you've been telling Gita, that I'm not allowed any more treatments until my bill has been paid?

MR HUTTON: That's correct, yes. (ADDRESSING THE BOARD MEMBERS) This is the lady I was telling you about, the one whose bill has been unpaid for five months now.

EVERYBODY TURNS TO LOOK AT BUBBLES.

BUBBLES: (DEFIANTLY) Why don't you take a photo? It lasts longer.

MR HUTTON: Mrs DeVere, will you please leave.

BUBBLES: Aren't you even going to introduce me?

MR HUTTON: (WEARILY) This is Mrs DeVere.

BUBBLES: Call me Bubbles.

MR HUTTON: Mrs DeVere, this is Mr Byfield, he's from Accounts.

BUBBLES: Yes . . .

MR HUTTON: Mr Shah, in charge of our legal side.

BUBBLES: Yes . . .

MR HUTTON: This is Miss Crozier.

BUBBLES: Yes . . .

MR HUTTON: And this is Sir Anthony Garfield, who's the owner.

BUBBLES' EARS PRICK UP.

BUBBLES: (SMILING) Oh the owner, oh, so Tony, it is a great pleasure to make your acquaintance.

SIR ANTHONY: Hello.

BUBBLES SITS ON THE EDGE OF THE MEETING TABLE BY SIR ANTHONY, WHO LOOKS HORRIFIED.

BUBBLES: (CALLS OUT) Champagne! (COSILY) So, Sir Tony, what sort of qualities do you look for in a woman?

SIR ANTHONY: You're sitting on my report!

BUBBLES: I do apologize, is this more comfortable?

SHE GETS UP FROM THE TABLE, AND INSTEAD SITS ON SIR ANTHONY'S LAP. SIR ANTHONY LOOKS VERY UNCOMFORTABLE.

SIR ANTHONY: No.

MR HUTTON: (STERNLY) Mrs DeVere, will you please leave?

BUBBLES TAKES SIR ANTHONY'S PEN AND THROWS IT ON THE FLOOR.

Champagne!

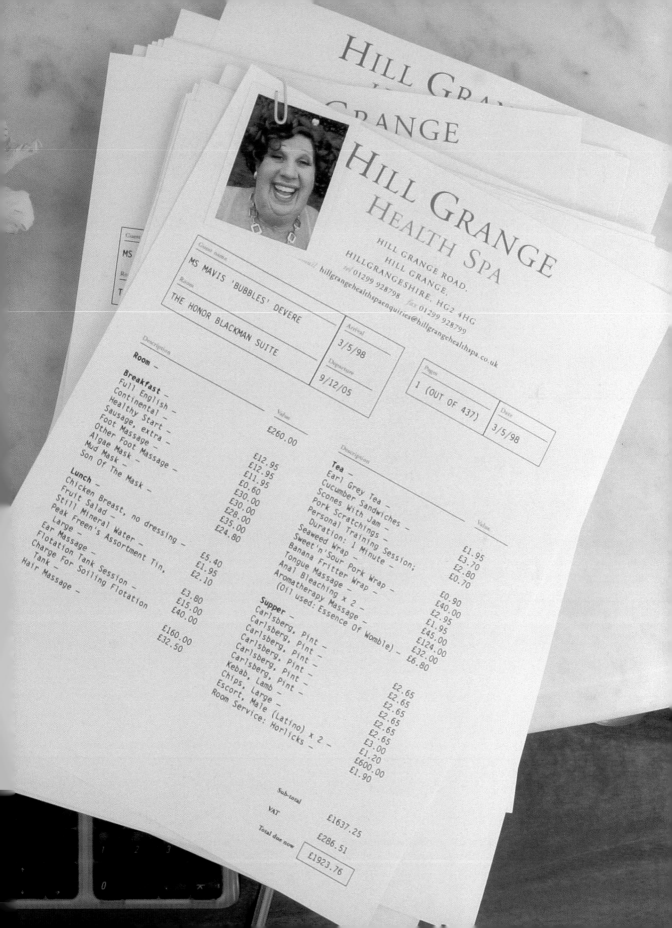

HILL GRANGE
HEALTH SPA

HILL GRANGE ROAD,
HILL GRANGE,
HILLGRANGESHIRE, HG2 4HG
tel 01299 928798   fax 01299 928799
hillgrangehealthspaenquiries@hillgrangehealthspa.co.uk

Guest name	
MS MAVIS 'BUBBLES' DEVERE	

Room	
THE HONOR BLACKMAN SUITE	

Arrival	3/5/98
Departure	9/12/05

Pages	1 (OUT OF 437)
Date	3/5/98

Description — Value

Room — £260.00

Breakfast
Full English —
Continental —
Healthy Start — £12.95
Sausage, extra — £12.95
Foot Massage — £11.95
Other Foot Massage — £0.60
Algae Mask — £30.00
Mud Mask — £28.00
Son Of The Mask — £35.00
— £24.80

Lunch
Chicken Breast, no dressing —
Fruit Salad —
Still Mineral Water — £5.40
Peak Freen's Assortment Tin, £1.95
Large — £2.10
Ear Massage —
Flotation Tank Session — £3.80
Charge For Soiling Flotation £15.00
Tank — £40.00
Hair Massage — £160.00
— £32.50

Tea
Earl Grey Tea —
Cucumber Sandwiches —
Scones With Jam — £1.95
Pork Scratchings — £3.70
Personal Training Session; £2.80
Duration: 1 Minute — £0.70
Seaweed Wrap —
Sweet 'n' Sour Pork Wrap — £0.90
Banana Fritter Wrap — £40.00
Tongue Massage — £2.95
Anal Bleaching x 2 — £1.95
Aromatherapy Massage — £45.00
(Oil used: Essence Of Womble) — £124.00
— £32.00
— £6.80

Supper
Carlsberg, Pint —
Carlsberg, Pint —
Carlsberg, Pint — £2.65
Carlsberg, Pint — £2.65
Carlsberg, Pint — £2.65
Kebab, Lamb — £2.65
Chips, Large — £2.65
Escort, Male (Latino) x 2 — £3.00
Room Service: Horlicks — £1.20
— £600.00
— £1.90

Sub-total — £1637.25

VAT — £286.51

Total due now — £1923.76

BUBBLES: Very well . . . oh . . . you dropped your pen . . .

SHE BENDS OVER, PRESENTING AN ENORMOUS BARE BUM TO SIR ANTHONY GARFIELD.

BUBBLES: I'm winking, darling . . .

MR HUTTON: (THROUGH HIS TEETH) Get out.

BUBBLES STANDS UP STRAIGHT, AND WHISPERS TO SIR ANTHONY BEFORE WALKING OUT.

BUBBLES: Meet me in the Jacuzzi in fifteen minutes.

MR MANN – RECORD SHOP

INT: RECORD SHOP. MR MANN ENTERS, AND SHUFFLES OVER TO THE COUNTER, WHERE ROY IS WAITING AS USUAL.

TOM V/O: It's nought o'clock and at this shop in Phlegm, Mr Mann is looking for a record. I myself own two records, both *No Parlez* by Paul Young.

I'm winking, darling . . .

ROY: Hello, how can I hel–?

MR MANN: (CUTTING HIM OFF) Hello, I would like to purchase a record of James Last, playing the hits of Nelly Furtado, on the banjo. And I would like a picture on the cover of James Last holding out his hands displaying stigmata.

ROY: Certainly . . . (WITHOUT PAUSING, ROY HOLDS UP A RECORD EXACTLY FITTING THAT DESCRIPTION AND PASSES IT TO MR MANN). Thank you.

MR MANN TAKES THE RECORD, AND STARTS TO WALK OUT OF THE SHOP. HE OBVIOUSLY HAS ANOTHER THOUGHT, AND STOPS.

MR MANN: Does it have the sleevenotes by Dr Graeme Garden?

ROY: Yes.

LOOKING SOMEWHAT DISAPPOINTED, MR MANN LEAVES.

Hello, I would like to

purchase a record of

James Last, playing the

hits of Nelly Furtado, on

the banjo. And I would

like a picture on the

cover of James La...

holding out his hands

displaying stigmata...

Certainly . . .

TWO LADIES IN RESTAURANT 3

INT: RESTAURANT. A WAITRESS IS SERVING THE SAME LADIES AS BEFORE.

RACHEL: Thank you. (TO HER FRIEND) So do you think you'll see Rupert again?

NICOLA: (SHARPLY) No, thank you.

RACHEL: Oh well, did you ever meet Simon's brother, Tom?

NICOLA: (SOFTENING) No, I don't think I did.

RACHEL: I think I've got a picture of them together somewhere . . . oh yes . . .

SHE PULLS OUT A POLAROID PHOTO OF MEN FROM THE WAIST DOWN, NAKED.

NICOLA: (APPRECIATIVELY) Oh, I can see the family resemblance.

MAGGIE AND JUDY — BRING-AND-BUY SALE

EXT: A VILLAGE FETE. WE SEE A GROUP OF BROWNIES BUSYING AROUND A STALL.

TOM V/O: Today in the charming village of Pox, the village green is host to a bring-and-buy sale. Last year's bring-and-buy sale was very successful and raised over one pound twenty.

JUDY AND MAGGIE ARE SIPPING FROM CUPS OF TEA.

JUDY: Slow today, isn't it?

MAGGIE: Yes.

A LITTLE BROWNIE WALKS UP TO MAGGIE AND JUDY WITH A PLATE OF BISCUITS.

JUDY: Oh, hello.

BROWNIE: Brown Owl's wondering if you'd like a gingerbread man each?

JUDY: Oh, thank you very much, how delightful, thank you.

MAGGIE: Thank you. Mmm, oh . . . delicious, did you make these?

THE BROWNIE HELPFULLY POINTS OUT A SMILING INDIAN GIRL.

BROWNIE: (BRIGHTLY) No, Anisha did.

MAGGIE INSTANTLY BEGINS TO HEAVE.

JUDY: No, Maggie, please . . . she's just a child . . .

MAGGIE VOMITS ALL OVER THE BROWNIE FOR SEVERAL SECONDS, PAUSES AND THEN VOMITS OVER HER AGAIN. THE BROWNIE STANDS THERE, TOO SHOCKED TO MOVE.

MAGGIE: (TO JUDY) So, did you get a chance to talk to Valerie about the Barnardo's job? (SHOOING THE STUNNED BROWNIE AWAY) Run along!

SEBASTIAN AND MICHAEL – CARELESS WHISPER

INT: THE PRIME MINISTER'S OFFICE, NO. 10. A PARTY IS IN FULL SWING, THE OFFICE LOOKING A LITTLE LIKE A DISCO AT A WEDDING. MICHAEL AND HIS WIFE ARE DANCING, SURROUNDED BY VARIOUS MINISTERS AND AIDES.

TOM V/O: At No. 10 the government is celebrating another election victory. I love an election, in fact I'm having one right now.

AN MP RAISES A GLASS TO MAKE A TOAST.

DEPUTY PRIME MINISTER: Here's to a third term. Wheeyyy!

O/S: Well done, everybody!

THE PRIME MINISTER HUGS HIS WIFE.

MICHAEL'S WIFE: (SMILING) You did it.

MICHAEL: *We* did it.

SEBASTIAN WALKS OVER AND BREAKS UP THEIR EMBRACE.

SEBASTIAN: What about me?

MICHAEL: Sebastian, thank you so much, you know I couldn't have done it without you.

SUDDENLY, THE MUSIC CHANGES DOWN A GEAR AS GEORGE MICHAEL'S Careless Whisper COMES ON. SUDDENLY LOOKING VERY PURPOSEFUL, SEBASTIAN PASSES HIS DRINK TO THE PRIME MINISTER'S WIFE, PULLS THE PRIME MINISTER CLOSE AND STARTS TO SLOW DANCE WITH HIM.

SEBASTIAN: (SEDUCTIVELY) This is nice, isn't it?

THE PRIME MINISTER LOOKS VERY AWKWARD, AND SEARCHES FOR EXCUSES TO BREAK THE EMBRACE.

MICHAEL: Erm, erm, yes, yes, it's going to be a very hectic day tomorrow, I'm gonna need your help, shepherding all the MPs out

SEBASTIAN: (SEXILY, WHISPERED) Sshhh.

MICHAEL: (SOLDIERING ON) Twenty-three new members, it's gonna be quite . . .

SEBASTIAN PUTS HIS FINGER ON MICHAEL'S LIPS, AND PULLS HIM EVEN CLOSER.

SEBASTIAN: Sshhh.

A GOVERNMENT WORKER WALKS OVER TO THEM.

GREGORY: Prime Minister,
I'd just like to say well . . .

SEBASTIAN WAVES HIM AWAY AND MOUTHS
'FUCK OFF'. THE MAN LEAVES. SEBASTIAN RUNS
HIS HANDS UP AND DOWN THE PRIME
MINISTER'S BODY AND BEGINS TO GO DOWN
ONTO HIS KNEES.

EPISODE Six

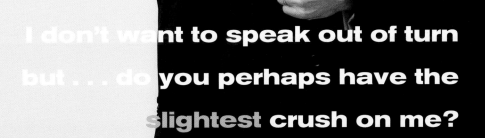

I don't want to speak out of turn
but . . . do you perhaps have the
slightest crush on me?

Fine . . . fine . . . fine . . .

MICHAEL: (FEELING SOMETHING STIRRING IN SEBASTIAN'S TROUSERS) Oh, oh, oh!

SEBASTIAN: Don't fight it, Prime Minister.

MICHAEL: This is a very . . . very long song, isn't it?

SEBASTIAN LEANS IN FOR A KISS. SUDDENLY, M PEOPLE'S 'MOVING ON UP' COMES ON AND THE PRIME MINISTER TAKES THE OPPORTUNITY TO DANCE AWAY. SEBASTIAN BURSTS INTO TEARS.

MICHAEL: I'll be back in a while, I'm going to talk to the Chancellor.

THE PRIME MINISTER NOTICES SEBASTIAN CRYING BITTERLY TO HIMSELF.

MICHAEL: Sebastian, are you alright?

SEBASTIAN: (REGAINING HIS COMPOSURE) Yeah I'm fine, I'm fine.

MICHAEL: (KINDLY) I don't want to speak out of turn but . . . do you perhaps have the slightest crush on me?

SEBASTIAN: (APPARENTLY CONFUSED AND EMBARRASSED) Oh oh oh, whatever gave you that idea? No no no, I just wanted to say well done.

MICHAEL: Oh, well, thank you, thank you.

Fine . . .

SEBASTIAN SUDDENLY GRABS THE PRIME MINISTER AND SNOGS HIM PASSIONATELY. HE BREAKS OFF LEAVING THE PRIME MINISTER STUNNED.

SEBASTIAN: Well done. (SPOTTING SOMEBODY ACROSS THE ROOM) Oh, hello!

LOU AND ANDY — SEASIDE

EXT: CAR PARK. LOU IS IN THE VAN, TRYING TO REVERSE INTO A PARKING SPACE. ANDY IS IN HIS WHEELCHAIR, HELPING HIM.

TOM V/O: As a special treat, Lou has taken Andy to the popular coastal town of Sphincter-on- Sea.

LOU: Right, tell me when . . .

LOU BEGINS TO REVERSE.

ANDY: Fine . . . fine . . . fine . . . (THE VAN CRASHES INTO THE CAR BEHIND). Fine . . .

IN THE VAN, LOU LOOKS DEFEATED, AND PUTS HIS HEAD ON THE STEERING WHEEL, SETTING OFF THE HORN.

WE CUT TO A SHOT OF LOU PUSHING ANDY ALONG THE SEAFRONT. AN ICE-CREAM MAN IS SETTING UP HIS STALL.

Wanna go swimming

ANDY: I wanna go swimming.

ANDY: Oh no, not today, it is very cold in there and I need someone else to help you get in and out and I haven't even brought your trunks, so the whole thing would be a right kerfuffle.

ANDY: Wanna go swimming.

LOU: I thought you didn't like swimming in the sea. I thought you said that the sea is a dark and brutal force that has dragged many an innocent to a watery grave?

ANDY: Yeah, I know.

LOU: Oh good, you stay there, I'll go and get you a choc-ice.

LOU LEAVES ANDY TO BUY A CHOC ICE FROM THE ICE-CREAM MAN. IN THE BACKGROUND, ANDY GETS OUT OF HIS CHAIR AND TAKES ALL OF HIS CLOTHES OFF.

LOU: Hello Mr Choc-ice-seller, erm, what types of choc ice have you got today? You've got your plain chocolate and your milk chocolate, and what's the main difference between the two? The milk one is creamier, it is sweeter isn't it.

ICE-CREAM MAN: Then there's the plain chocolate . . .

BEHIND LOU, WE SEE ANDY RUNNING INTO THE SEA, NAKED.

LOU: The plain chocolate is slightly darker, has a bitter edge to it, it's not to everybody's taste but some people do prefer the plain over the milk, it's very interesting that. If you had to pick between the two what would you choose? You'd choose the plain one, alright well let me try one plain one then. There you go. That's a nice one, that. That's the best choc ice you can get, alright, thanks a lot. (ANDY RUNS BACK TO HIS CHAIR, NAKED, AND SITS DOWN JUST BEFORE LOU TURNS ROUND TO HAND HIM HIS CHOC ICE) Here we are, my young friend.

LOU RESUMES PUSHING ANDY ALONG THE SEAFRONT. THERE IS A PAUSE.

LOU: Is there a reason why you're naked?

TOM V/O: And so another remarkable series of Little Britain comes to an end. If you have enjoyed the series and you see me in the street, you may like to come up to me and caress my thighs and buttocks, good pie!

I thought you didn't like swimming in the sea. I thought you said that the sea is a dark and brutal force that has dragged many an innocent to a watery grave?

Yeah, I know.

THE comic relief sketches

TOM V/O: Britain, Britain, Britain. It's been called heaven on earth, and it's easy to see why. Ribena is plentiful, shoelaces are available in different languages, and there's a new Fred Bassett cartoon strip in the *Daily Mail* every day. But let's not forget the people of Britain. For it is they what make it good and nice, and it is that lot that we look at today. Yippee-doo-da!

LOU AND ANDY — GEORGE MICHAEL

EXT. DAY. COUNCIL ESTATE. LOU IS PUSHING ANDY IN WHEELCHAIR.

TOM V/O: After an enjoyable day sitting on a bench, Lou is taking Andy home for his dinner.

THEY MEET A WOMAN THEY KNOW, WHO STOPS TO SAY HELLO. ANDY GRABS ONE OF HER BREASTS.

INT. BATHROOM IN ANDY'S HOUSE. ANDY SITS ON TOILET, EATING CRISPS. LOU STANDS BY HIM, HOLDING TOILET ROLL.

LOU: Now, I know it's your birthday coming up, and I thought we could do something special, so I've booked a table up the Harvester.

ANDY: Yeah, I know.

LOU: Is there anyone you'd like me to invite?

ANDY: George Michaels.

LOU: You want me to invite George Michaels?

ANDY: Yeah.

LOU: We don't know him.

ANDY: Yeah, I know.

LOU: Well, I don't think he'd come. Anyway, I thought you didn't like George Michaels. I thought you said that 'Jesus to a Child' aside, you found his output emotionally vapid.

ANDY: Yeah, I know.

LOU: Let's invite someone else instead. How about your brother Declan?

ANDY: George Michaels.

LOU: (HANDING ANDY SOME TOILET PAPER) Oh my sweet saviour.

INT. CHEAP-LOOKING RESTAURANT. LOU AND ANDY SITTING AT TABLE.

LOU: (SHOWING MENU TO ANDY) So birthday boy, what would you like for your mains?

ANDY: (POINTS AT MENU WITHOUT LOOKING) That one.

LOU: Ice cream. And what do you want for your pudding?

ANDY: (POINTS AGAIN WITHOUT LOOKING) That one.

LOU: Garlic bread. OK. (LOOKS AT HIS WATCH) Oh, I must just get something out of the van. Wait there. (GETS UP AND GOES TO DOOR TO LET IN GEORGE MICHAEL) Well . . . hello Mr Michaels. Well, well. Well, you know . . . well you're here. Thank you for coming. He's gonna be chuffed to bits.

GEORGE: That's quite all right. You know, I like to do my bit.

LOU: Very nice of you. Andy! I've got a surprise for you. This is George Michaels.

ANDY PAYS GEORGE NO ATTENTION.

GEORGE: Hello, Andy. (HOLDS OUT HIS HAND BUT ANDY DOESN'T TAKE IT) Er, nice to meet you. (PAUSE) Happy birthday. (PAUSE)

ANDY: I don't like him. I want him to go. I prefer Tony Hadley.

LOU: I'm sorry Mr Michaels. I'm sorry. (USHERS GEORGE TO THE DOOR)

ANDY: Tell him 'Jesus to a Child' aside I find his output emotionally vapid.

LOU: Did you get that, George?

GEORGE: Yeah, thank you.

PRIME MINISTER AND SEBASTIAN — THE ADMIRAL

EXT. DAY. NO. 10 DOWNING STREET. CHAUFFEUR OPENS DOOR FOR PM TO GET OUT OF CAR. SEBASTIAN EMBRACES PM AS PRESS PHOTOGRAPHERS TAKE PICTURES.

TOM V/O: At number 10 Downing Street the Prime Minister has returned after a week away at the NATO conference.

INT. PM'S OFFICE. PM AND CHIEF ADMIRAL SITTING EITHER SIDE OF DESK.

TOM V/O: The first meeting of the day is with the Chief Admiral.

ADMIRAL: The problem is, Prime Minister, that Polaris is rapidly becoming obsolete. Unless we replace it soon, we shall be in very dangerous waters.

CAMERA PANS BACK TO REVEAL SEBASTIAN STANDING NEXT TO PM.

PRIME MINISTER: I have already explained, I cannot commit any more money to defence.

ADMIRAL: I urge you, Prime Minister, to come down to Portsmouth, spend some time on board one of our vessels to see for yourself.

SEBASTIAN: Very clever.

ADMIRAL: Excuse me.

SEBASTIAN: What you're doing. Very clever.

ADMIRAL: I don't follow.

SEBASTIAN: Get him on the boat, plaster him with rum: 'Oh, sorry, I thought that was my hammock!'

ADMIRAL: What?

SEBASTIAN: I know what you sailors get up to.

PRIME MINISTER: Thank you, Sebastian. Continue, Chief Admiral.

ADMIRAL: Oh, well, I think, sir, you'll be shocked by the state the fleet's in. I'd like formally to extend an invitation . . .

SEBASTIAN: I bet that's not all you're extending!

ADMIRAL: . . . to come on board one of our ships.

SEBASTIAN: (POINTING AT ADMIRAL) Oh, she's so blatant!

ADMIRAL: I don't know what you mean.

SEBASTIAN: Oh, don't play the innocent with me. (PRANCES OVER TO ADMIRAL) Mincing in here in uniform – 'Oh, Prime Minister, we need bigger missiles'. Nice try, dear.

PRIME MINISTER: That's enough, Sebastian. (SEBASTIAN WALKS BACK TO HIS SIDE, SULKILY) I'll have a look in the diary for next week.

SEBASTIAN: We're busy.

PRIME MINISTER: I'm sure we have time for the Chief Admiral.

SEBASTIAN: Well, if you wanna go, go. But don't come running back to me asking for Preparation H. I shan't be interested.

PRIME MINISTER: Sebastian, I think you should leave.

SEBASTIAN: (WALKING TOWARDS DOOR, ARMS FOLDED, TOSSING HEAD) Whatever! (TURNS ROUND) Bye, Prime Minister. Bye, Cap'n Birdseye.

PM MOVES TOWARDS SEBASTIAN, WHO RUNS OUT OF ROOM.

PRIME MINISTER: (SITTING ON DESK BY ADMIRAL) I'm so sorry.

ADMIRAL: We wouldn't have to share the hammock. (PUTS HAND ON PM'S THIGH)

JUDY AND MAGGIE – SCOUTS

EXT. DAY. CHURCH. GROUP OF CUB SCOUTS SING IN GARDEN BEDECKED WITH BALLOONS AND PENNANTS.

TOM V/O: The cub-scout movement was founded by Lord Baden-Powell, who took much of his inspiration from *The Jungle Book* by Walt Disney.

WOMAN SCOUT LEADER [AKELA] WALKS PAST WITH PLATE OF SCONES TOWARDS MAGGIE AND JUDY.

MAGGIE: Aren't they wonderful, Judy?

JUDY: Oh yes, delightful, Maggie.

WOMAN: Hello.

MAGGIE: Hello Akela.

WOMAN: Would you care for a scone? (HOLDS OUT PLATE)

JUDY: Yes, that would be lovely.

MAGGIE: Thank you. (THEY START EATING SCONES) Mmm, delicious. Did you make these?

WOMAN: No, Baloo did. (POINTS TO BLACK WOMAN SITTING BEHIND TEA STALL)

MAGGIE LOOKS ILL, MAKES STRANGE NOSIES.

JUDY: Maggie, Maggie, Maggie, oh . . .

A RIVER OF VOMIT GUSHES FROM MAGGIE'S MOUTH, DRENCHING THE SCOUTS, WHO STOP SINGING.

MAGGIE: Don't stop on my account.

VICKY POLLARD ON TRISHA

INT. TV STUDIO. TRISHA AND SOUNDMAN STAND BY SEATED KEN ON STAGE IN FRONT OF AUDIENCE. MUSIC STARTS, SOUNDMAN LEAVES AND TRISHA SITS DOWN.

TOM V/O: If you or your family have a sensitive problem, the best way to deal with it is to go on television and talk about it.

TV CREDITS ROLL: PART 2 OF TRISHA: FAMILIES REUNITED.

TRISHA: Welcome back, welcome back. Today we're looking for lost loved ones. Now, Ken, tell us your story.

KEN: Well, um, 14 years ago, I had a daughter, but I've lost touch with her, and I'd really like to see her again.

TRISHA: Now, do you know her name?

KEN: Um, well, I didn't get the mother's name, but I think she called our daughter Victoria.

TRISHA: Right, well, we've got a bit of a surprise for you today. What you don't know is that we've managed to track your daughter down.

KEN: My God I don't believe it.

TRISHA: Yes, she's here today. She doesn't know why she's here yet but please welcome Vicky Pollard. (WALKS OVE R TO AUDIENCE AS VICKY COMES ON STAGE TO APPLAUSE AND SITS IN HER CHAIR) Hi Vicky. Now you don't actually know why you're here today, do you?

VICKY: No but yeah but no but yeah . . . but is it cos you're doing Teens in Trouble right cos I not never even done nuffin' cos let me tell you the whole thing right cos Michelle Bingham who's a complete bitch anyway and has been completely going around saying that I went into Shelley Stockwell's bag and nicked a bottle of Cinzano but I never but I did but only cos you're not actually supposed to have alcohol on the school grounds actually and I was gonna give it to Miss Turvy but I forgot and drank it and I only got found out cos I was getting off with Asif Shah behind the language lab and I was sick in his mouth.

TRISHA: No, that's not why you're here today.

VICKY: You've been talkin' you've been talkin' Destiny Platt haven't you cos you know Destiny Platt right?

TRISHA: No.

VICKY: She ain't even got nuffin' to do with it anyway so leave her out of it . . . stop gettin' involved Trisha Goddard you're such a mixer . . . I know why I'm here it's cos you're doin' I've Had Two Babies and I'm Only Twelve . . . you're well out of order cos I was thirteen when I had my second child anyway if you've been talkin' Aaron Peel cos let me tell you Aaron Peel right cos listen to this Trish . . .

TRISHA: No, no, just listen to me for just a second (GESTURING WITH HANDS).

VICKY: Talk to the face the hand ain't listening . . . Aaron Peel is a totally batty boy and he ain't got no pubes and he's well out of order cos he's been completely going around saying that I like smoke and drank when I was pregnant but all I did was smoke like two packs of fags a day and drank like fifty pints of Snakebites a night but apart from that I never done nuffin' so you can shut up you total minger!

TRISHA: You're not in trouble, you're not in trouble. You're here for something nice, Vicky.

VICKY: Totally really?

TRISHA: Yes.

VICKY: No I know it's cos you're doin' I Wanna Be a Lapdancer and you want me on it cos I'm like totally fit and all the girls in the audience are gonna be like well jealous cos they're such ugly bitches and all the blokes are gonna be like yeah go for it we wanna see you up Spearmint Rhino cos they wanna do me and they've probably got a stiffy anyway just lookin' at me and my leggings cos they can all see my camel's hoof.

TRISHA: No, Vicky. Ken, I believe there was something you wanted to say.

KEN: (LOOKING STUNNED AND HORRIFIED) Yeah, I wanna DNA test.

VICKY: I'm gonna be a lapdancer everybody.

VICKY STARTS LAP-DANCE ROUTINE, STRIPPING OFF HER TOP AND GYRATING OVER KEN, AS AUDIENCE CLAP.

TRISHA: Vicky, no. No, no, no, no.

VICKY: Come on Trisha, let's do a lesbian show.

TRISHA: No, Vicky. This is your dad.

VICKY MOVES QUICKLY AWAY FROM KEN, LOOKING DISGUSTED.

VICKY: What? Eergh! You complete and utter pervert! My God, what are you . . . some sort of paediatrician or something.

KEN: No, no, you've got it wrong, cos you see I came on this show . . .

VICKY: You're well out of order.

TRISHA: Uh, we're going to go to a break.

VICKY: You're well gonna get beatings for this Trisha Goddard!

VICKY PUSHES OVER HER CHAIR.

BANK — COMIC RELIEF FUN RUN

EXT. DAY. MIDWEST BANK. PENSIONER SEALS HER DOG'S EXCREMENT IN PLASTIC BAG AND PUTS IT ON BODY OF MAN ON PASSING STRETCHER.

TOM V/O: Banks in Britain are notoriously generous. If you become overdrawn, they let you keep the money for free.

INT. BANK OFFICE BANK CLERK CAROL BEER SITS BEHIND DESK WITH COMPUTER. BANK MANAGER WALKS IN, TALKING TO SOMEONE OUTSIDE.

BANK MANAGER: Yeah, no that's Miss Whatsit. Tell her I've frozen her account, OK? (SMILES AT CAROL) Hi, how are you? (CAROL IS STONY-FACED) Um, me and Craig and Sharita thought we might do this fun run in aid of Comic Relief, and wondered if you fancied taking part?

CAROL: (TYPES ON KEYBOARD) Computer says when is it?

BANK MANAGER: The fourteenth. It's a Sunday.

CAROL: (TYPES ON KEYBOARD AGAIN) Computer says what time?

BANK MANAGER: Eleven.

CAROL: (TYPES ON KEYBOARD YET AGAIN) Computer says how far is it?

BANK MANAGER: It's just five miles.

CAROL: (PRESSES ONE KEY) Computer says no.

DAFFYD THOMAS — SIR ELTON JOHN

INT. ROOM IN POSH HOTEL. DAFFYD SITS BY HIMSELF, HOLDING NOTEPAD AND PENCIL.

TOM V/O: Meanwhile, rural gay Daffyd Thomas has come to London's ritzy Ritz Hotel to do an interview for his local paper.

DAFFYD: (LOOKING IMPATIENT) We never had this with Aled Jones. Oh, come on. (CALLS OUT TO OPEN DOORWAY) Are you gonna be long?

ELTON JOHN WALKS THROUGH DOORWAY AND COMES OVER TO DAFFYD, WHO STANDS UP TO SHAKE HANDS.

ELTON: Elton John. How are you?

DAFFYD: Yes, uh . . . Daffyd Thomas, the only gay in the village. Please take a seat.

THEY SIT.

ELTON: What's this for exactly?

DAFFYD: This is the big one. It's the Llandewi Breffi Gazette. (HOLDS UP A COPY OF THE NEWSPAPER) OK, so first things first. Let's get a little bit of background. Um, are you married?

ELTON: No.

DAFFYD: Any kids?

ELTON: No.

DAFFYD: I've often seen you around and about with this chap David Furness. Is he one of your nephews?

ELTON: No

DAFFYD: (WRITES IN NOTEPAD) 'Close friend.' Okey-dokey. Now, let's get on and talk

I've often seen you around and about with this chap David Furness. Is he one of your nephews?

about your work. Now, when it comes to writing a song, Bernie Taupin, he writes the lyrics, and you write the music. Does it come quickly or do you find yourself staying up at night and bashing one out?

ELTON: No, I've always come quickly, actually, yes.

DAFFYD: Now, when you're not writing or recording, you like to do live concerts, don't you?

ELTON: Yes.

DAFFYD: Yes, in fact, you've recently been playing in Las Vegas. Do you enjoy filling Celine Dion's slot?

ELTON: I wish I could say yes, but no.

DAFFYD: Now, you've started to write musicals. You've done Aida, you've done Lion King, and most recently Billy Elliot. Would you say you were somebody who had a theatrical bent?

ELTON: Definitely.

DAFFYD: (WRITES IN NOTEPAD) 'Definitely. Very theatrical.' I've always thought you were. Now, some of the people in the village have suggested questions. Old Ma Evans, who works in the post office on a Tuesday – you know her – she says you're a very big football supporter and you were the chairman of Watford Football Club.

ELTON: That's correct, yes.

DAFFYD: That's right. What she wants to

THE *comic relief sketches*

know is did you let the manager make the decisions or would you come down and pull someone off at half-time?

ELTON: If only. No, I would never interfere with the manager.

DAFFYD: I'll take your word for it. So, you like tennis, you like football, are you into water sports?

ELTON: Not really, no, no.

KNOCK AT THE DOOR. VOICE CALLS OUT 'ROOM SERVICE' AND SPANISH MAID ENTERS WITH TEA TROLLEY.

SPANISH WAITER: Here we are. Now I have . . . afternoon tea, fairy cake, chocolate éclair . . . (RECOGNIZES ELTON) Ooh, Señor Elton John! I am loving your music. (SINGS) 'I want love, but of a different kind . . . It's a little bit funny, this feeling inside' (POINTING AT HIS BUM) 'Are you ready, are your ready for bum?' (WIGGLING HIS BUM) 'Yes, I am, yes I am'. (OFFERS ELTON CAKE) Cream horn? (KNEELS BY

That's right. What she wants to know is did you let the manager make the decisions or would you come down and pull someone off at half-time?

ELTON) Señor John, you're so attractive and magnifico. Sexo with me . . . telefono cuatro, cuatro, cuatro, ocho, ocho, ocho . . . Ooh-ooh, ooh-ooh, ooh-ooh! (MINCES BACKWARDS OUT OF ROOM, WAVING GOODBYE)

ELTON: She was camp, wasn't she? Oh, dear.

DAFFYD: I didn't really notice. (LOOKS AT NOTEPAD) You're very well known for your generosity. Do you enjoy splashing out on David?

ELTON: Always, yeah.

DAFFYD: And you're always giving, aren't you? Give, give, give. But do you like to receive?

ELTON: I prefer to give, actually.

DAFFYD: You prefer to give. Yes. Now, I know you have given a lot of interviews today, but I'd like to ask you one more thing. You've had a very successful career. So successful, in fact, that you've been knighted by the Queen. Have you met many queens?

ELTON: Loads. More than I could ever have imagined.

DAFFYD: Really? Very successful, aren't you? And I should imagine it would be very nerve-wracking meeting Her Majesty. What's it like kneeling before the Queen? Do you get a lump in the throat?

ELTON: Hopefully.

DAFFYD: (WRITES IN NOTEPAD) 'With a bit of luck, gets a lump.' Well, that is all my questions. Thank you ever so much for having me here today, Elton Jones. (THEY

STAND UP AND SHAKE HANDS) I'm gonna go now, back to my home in Llandewi Breffi, which is a lovely village. In fact, you live in a nice village, don't you?

ELTON: I do, yeah.

DAFFYD: In Berkshire?

ELTON: Yes, that's right.

DAFFYD: Yes, I've heard it's very nice, very picturesque.

ELTON: It is, yeah.

DAFFYD: In fact, there's a lot of nice cottages there. I might come down and explore them.

ELTON: Well, I don't think that's a good idea.

DAFFYD: Why not?

ELTON: Cos I'm the only gay in that village. (WALKS OUT OF ROOM)

DAFFYD: (SITS DOWN AGAIN) A bit of overreaction, I thought.

RESTAURANT – HUBBA BUBBA

INT. SMART RESTAURANT. GENTLEMAN SITTING AT TABLE READING A MENU. WAITER WALKS OVER.

TOM V/O: A lunch order is being taken.

WAITER: Is sir ready to order?

MAN: (IN DRAWLING VOICE) Yes, I'll have the quail's egg salad to start.

WAITER: And to follow?

MAN: The lobster thermidor, with steamed broccoli and sugar snap peas.

WAITER: Thank you, sir. (STARTS TO LEAVE)

MAN: And some hubba bubba.

WAITER: Any particular flavour, sir?

MAN: Let chef decide.

WAITER LEAVES. MAN'S HEAD SLUMPS FORWARD.

DENNIS WATERMAN – CHITTY CHITTY BANG BANG

INT. THEATRICAL AGENT JEREMY RENT'S OFFICE. JEREMY SITS AT DESK, HOLDING AND KISSING BABY.

TOM V/O: Meanwhile in Troot, theatrical agent Jeremy Rent is looking after his baby granddaughter. I myself love babies and have over 300 at home.

RECEPTIONIST BUZZES JEREMY.

RECEPTIONIST: Dennis Waterman here to see you.

JEREMY: Oh, lovely. Send him in.

DENNIS WALKS IN CARRYING A HUGE PIECE OF TOAST, AND SITS OPPOSITE JEREMY.

DENNIS: (IN BOY'S HIGH-PITCHED VOICE) Hello. I've brought you some more toast.

JEREMY: Hello there. That's very . . . thoughtful of you. (TAKES TOAST, WHICH IMMEDIATELY BECOMES NORMAL SIZED) Here's some toast, look at this. Do excuse me, I've been left holding the baby somewhat.

DENNIS: I like babies.

JEREMY: Well, yes, this is my new granddaughter, Clarissa. I'm just looking after her while my daughter goes to an audition.

DENNIS: Ooh, can I hold her.

JEREMY: If you're very, very careful, OK? Two hands, and support the head.

GIVES DENNIS BABY, WHICH TURNS INTO AN OLD MAN.

DENNIS: Ooh, she's big for her age. ('BABY' GURGLES) I think she needs feeding.

JEREMY: There you go, you can do it. (PASSES HIM A BOTTLE, WHICH IS HUGE TO DENNIS. DENNIS FEEDS 'BABY') Now, I've had a call from the chaps at the Palladium, and they'd like to offer you the part of Caractacus Potts in Chitty Chitty Bang Bang.

DENNIS: Have you, er, got her dummy?

JEREMY: There you go.

GIVES DENNIS DUMMY, WHICH BECOMES OUTSIZED. DENNIS PUTS IT IN 'BABY'S' MOUTH.

DENNIS: Oh, that's nice. Chitty Chitty Bang Bang. Yes, I took my daughter, who was in EastEnders, to see it. So, they want me to star in it, write the theme tune, sing the theme tune . . .

JEREMY: Oh, no, no, no. They've already written all the music, haven't they? You know: (SINGS) 'Bang bang, chitty chitty bang bang'.

DENNIS: Oh, yeah, I remember it. (SINGS) 'Bang bang chitty chitty bang bang. Doo doo doo doo doo. A musical based on the book by James Bond creator Ian Fleming. Doo doo doo doo doo. You'll believe a car

can fly, unless you're sitting in the stalls, when you can see clearly its mechanical arm.'

JEREMY: (WRINKLING NOSE) Oh, I think the baby's nappy needs changing.

DENNIS: Oh no, that's me.

FLORENCE AND EMILY – ROBBIE WILLIAMS

EXT. OUTSIDE 'EMILY'S THINGS', A LADIES' DRESS SHOP.

TOM V/O: Transvestism in Little Britain is now more prevalent than ever, with nearly 50 per cent of the population dressed as women.

INT. INSIDE SHOP WITH EMILY AND FLORENCE.

FLORENCE: Oh, Emily, it was such a wonderful idea of yours to open up this ladies' shop.

EMILY: Oh, thank you Florence, my dear. Yes, I think it's very important that ladies like us . . . we are ladies, aren't we?

FLORENCE: Oh, yes, Emily, we are certainly two of them.

THE comic relief sketches

EMILY: Yes, I think it's important that ladies like us have somewhere we can go where we can buy our ladies' things – our little lace handkerchiefs, our parasols, our general ladies' . . . (IN DEEP MAN'S VOICE) shit.

DOOR OPENS AND ROBBIE WILLIAMS WALKS IN.

FLORENCE: Oh, Emily, a customer.

ROBBIE: Hi fellahs!

EMILY AND FLORENCE LOOK BEHIND AS IF LOOKING FOR MEN.

EMILY: Hello. Yes, we are ladies.

FLORENCE: Welcome to our ladies' shop.

ROBBIE: This used to be Burton's, right?

EMILY: Oh, yes, that's right.

ROBBIE: I used to get all my clothes from here. But it's all right, there's a Mr Byrite on the corner. I'll just go there.

EMILY: Oh no, no, no. (LAUGHS AND TAKES HIS ARM) I'm sure we can find something for you. We've got a shy one. (PATS HIS BOTTOM AND TAKES HIM BEHIND SCREEN) Go on, let's get these trousers off.

ROBBIE: No!

TROUSERS THROWN ON TOP OF SCREEN.

FLORENCE: Can I give you a hand, Emily?

EMILY: Oh, no thank you, my dear, I'm fine.

ROBBIE: Not my thong!

THONG THROWN TO FLORENCE.

EMILY: Let's get these knickers on you dear.

PAUSE. EMILY EMERGES FROM BEHIND SCREEN.

EMILY: Florence, may I present to you a new lady friend of mine, Miss Roberta Williams?

ROBBIE EMERGES, DRESSED IN LADIES' CLOTHES.

FLORENCE: Oh, someone's going to be breaking a few men's hearts.

ROBBIE: Really?

EMILY: Yes, you'll be quite the belle of the ball.

ROBBIE: It's funny, I do actually feel comfortable dressed like this. (TOUCHES HIS 'BUST') It's like I feel myself for the very first time. (IN LADY'S VOICE) Yes, indeed, ladies, I could get quite used to this. (WALKS TO DOOR) Thank you very much. Au revoir!

EXT. SHOP. ROBBIE WALTZES OFF WITH PARASOL RAISED, OGLING PASSING MEN.

ROBBIE: (LAUGHING) I'm a lady!

EMILY: (IN SHOP DOORWAY, IN MAN'S VOICE) Bloody poof!

LOU AND ANDY – ATHLETIC GROUND

EXT. DAY. ATHLETIC GROUND. TWO ATHLETES RUN ON TRACK. LOU PUSHES ANDY IN WHEELCHAIR.

TOM V/O: It's half-past Oliver, and Lou has taken Andy to Herby athletics track.

LOU: Right. OK. Now. I'm just gonna do a few laps today, cos I need to train for this fun run.

ANDY: (EATING BAG OF SWEETS) Yeah, I know.

LOU: If we raise enough money, we're gonna be able to buy you one of these new motorized electrical wheelchairs thingamajigabies.

ANDY: Yeah, I know.

LOU: Right, you just wait here. I won't be long.

ANDY: Fine, fine.

LOU STARTS WARMING UP ON TRACK. UNSEEN, IN

BACKGROUND, LOU POLE VAULTS OVER THE BAR AND THEN DOES A BACK FLIP.

TOM V/O: And so we leave our friends in Little Britain. If you have enjoyed tonight's episode, you might like to make sweet, beautiful love to me as a small way of saying thank you. Goodguy.

Little Britain series two

Written and performed
  by Matt Lucas and David Walliams
Director: Matt Lipsey
Producer: Geoff Posner
Executive Producers: Myfanwy Moore,
  Jon Plowman
Script Editor: Rob Brydon
Music: David Arnold
Locations: Thomas Howard,
  Caroline McCarthy
Sound: Alex Thompson, St Clair Davis,
  Jem Whippey
Make Up and Hair Designer:
  Lisa Cavalli-Green
Make-up Assistants: Nicola Coleman,
  Suzi Munachen
Costume Designer: Annie Hardinge
Costume Assistant: Sheena Gunn
Director of Photography:
  Francis de Groote
Production Manager: Francis Gilson
Production Designer: Dennis de Groote
Editor: Mykola Pawluk
Production Executive: Jez Nightingale
Script Supervisors: Chrissie Bibby,
  Katie Collins
Production Co-Ordinator: Charlotte Lamb
Production Team: Kelley James,
  Sarah Hollingsworth
Dubbing Mixer: Rob Butler-Biggs
1st Assistant Director: Sam Dawking
Assistant Director: Bart Bailey, Paul Cathie
Art Director: Andrew Gates

Casting: Tracey Gillham
Camera Team: Joe Smyth, Jonathon
  Tomes, Jimmy Ward
Cameras: Dave Bowden, Peter Welch
Studio Resource Manager:
  Michael Matheson
Vision Mixer: Barbara Hicks
Stage Manager: Caroline Caley
Prop Master: Dean Humphrey
Props: Keith Warwick, Leo Thompson,
  John Paul Rock, Simon Naylor,
  John Helmsley
Production Buyer: Jac Hymen
Stunt Co-ordinator: Andreas Petrides
With thanks to Pozzitive Television
With the voice of Tom Baker
Special Guests: Anthony Head,
  Geraldine James

Featuring

Jaygann Ayeh, Robert Blythe, Marlon
Bulger, Joanna Burford, James Cash,
Charubala Chokshi, Joanne Condon,
Michael Elliott, Howell Evans, Kerry Foxe,
David Foxxe, Steve Furst, Stirling Gallacher,
David Garfield, Georgie Glen, Mike Hayward,
Kobna Holdbrook-Smith, Cherylee Houston,
Ruth Jones, Patricia Kane, Faith Kent,
Geoff Leesley, Janette Legge, Joan Linder,
Jennie Lucey, David Morris,
Samantha Power, Paul Putner,
Ted Robbins, Leelo Ross, Antonia Whillans

Matt and David would like to thank Richard Curtis, Kevin Cahill,
Peter Bennett-Jones and all at Comic Relief, as well as Sir Elton John,
George Michael, Robbie Williams, Simon Callow, Trisha Goddard,
Gareth Carrivick and everyone who so kindly gave up their time to work
on the Little Britain Comic Relief Special. If you would like to contribute to
Comic Relief, please call **08457 910 910** or go to **www.rednoseday.com**

**The complete Series 1 and 2 are also available on DVD, and the two
original Radio 4 series are available on BBC Audio CD and cassette
and in a special tin gift set with bonus discs.**

If you enjoyed this book, why not buy other books, such as 'Catcher in the Rye', 'The Da Vinci Code' and Harry bloody Potter.